TO:

_____

FROM:

_____

DATE:

_____

SIMPLE
BLESSINGS

Freeman-Smith, a division of Worthy Media, Inc.

134 Franklin Road, Suite 200, Brentwood, Tennessee 37027

The quoted ideas expressed in this book (but not Scripture verses) are not, in all cases, exact quotations, as some have been edited for clarity and brevity. In all cases, the author has attempted to maintain the speaker's original intent. In some cases, quoted material for this book was obtained from secondary sources, primarily print media. While every effort was made to ensure the accuracy of these sources, the accuracy cannot be guaranteed. For additions, deletions, corrections, or clarifications in future editions of this text, please write Freeman-Smith.

Scripture quotations are taken from:

The Holy Bible, King James Version (KJV)

The Holy Bible, New International Version (NIV) Copyright © 1973, 1978, 1984, by International Bible Society. Used by permission of Zondervan Publishing House. All rights reserved.

The Holy Bible, New King James Version (NKJV) Copyright © 1982 by Thomas Nelson, Inc. Used by permission.

Holy Bible, New Living Translation, (NLT) copyright © 1996. Used by permission of Tyndale House Publishers, Inc., Wheaton, Illinois 60189. All rights reserved.

The Message (MSG)- This edition issued by contractual arrangement with NavPress, a division of The Navigators, U.S.A. Originally published by NavPress in English as THE MESSAGE: The Bible in Contemporary Language copyright 2002-2003 by Eugene Peterson. All rights reserved.

New Century Version®. (NCV) Copyright © 1987, 1988, 1991 by Word Publishing, a division of Thomas Nelson, Inc. All rights reserved. Used by permission.

The New American Standard Bible®, (NASB) Copyright © 1960, 1962, 1963, 1968, 1971, 1972, 1973, 1975, 1977, 1995 by The Lockman Foundation. Used by permission.

The Holman Christian Standard Bible™ (HCSB) Copyright © 1999, 2000, 2001 by Holman Bible Publishers. Used by permission.

Cover Design by Scott Williams/Richmond & Williams

Page Layout by Bart Dawson

ISBN 978-1-60587-520-0 (special edition)

ISBN 978-1-60587-521-7

Printed in China

1 2 3 4 5—RRD—17 16 15 14 13

SIMPLE
BLESSINGS

Table of Contents

Introduction

Today and every day, the sun rises upon a world filled with God's presence and His love. As Christians, we have so many reasons to rejoice: The Father is in His heaven, His love is everlasting, and we, His children, are blessed beyond measure. Yet sometimes we find ourselves distracted by the demands, the frustrations, and the uncertainties of daily life. But even during our darkest days, God never leaves us for an instant. And even when our hopes are dimmed, God's light still shines brightly. As followers of God's Son, we are called to search for that light—and to keep searching for it as long as we live.

This text celebrates the simple blessings that flow from the loving heart of God. These pages contain inspirational Bible verses, thought-provoking quotations, and brief essays—all of which can lift your spirits and guide your path.

So today, as you embark upon the next step of your life's journey, count as many blessings as you can, and think of ways that you can find—and share—the promises that God has made to those who choose to follow in the footsteps of His Son. When you do, you'll discover that joy is like honey: It's hard to spread it around without getting some on yourself.

CHAPTER 1

Simple Blessings

I will make them and the area around My hill a blessing; I will send down showers in their season—showers of blessing.

—Ezekiel 34:26 HCSB

Many of life's blessings are so obvious and so simple. Yet, we often take them for granted.

If you sat down and began counting your blessings, how long would it take? The answer, of course, is, "A very, very long time!"

Your blessings include life, freedom, family, friends, talents, and possessions, for starters. But, your greatest blessing—a gift that is yours for the asking—is God's gift of salvation through Christ Jesus.

Today, begin making a list of your blessings. You most certainly will not be able to make a complete list, but take a few moments and jot down as many blessings as you can. Then give thanks to the giver of all good things: God. His love for you is

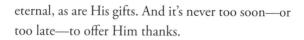
eternal, as are His gifts. And it's never too soon—or too late—to offer Him thanks.

MORE IMPORTANT IDEAS ABOUT GOD'S BLESSINGS

God's kindness is not like the sunset—brilliant in its intensity, but dying every second. God's generosity keeps coming and coming and coming.

Bill Hybels

When you and I are related to Jesus Christ, our strength and wisdom and peace and joy and love and hope may run out, but His life rushes in to keep us filled to the brim. We are showered with blessings, not because of anything we have or have not done, but simply because of Him.

Anne Graham Lotz

Blessings can either humble us and draw us closer to God or allow us to become full of pride and self-sufficiency.

Jim Cymbala

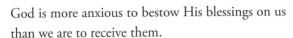

God is more anxious to bestow His blessings on us than we are to receive them.

St. Augustine

God blesses us in spite of our lives and not because of our lives.

Max Lucado

Think of the blessings we so easily take for granted: Life itself; preservation from danger; every bit of health we enjoy; every hour of liberty; the ability to see, to hear, to speak, to think, and to imagine all this comes from the hand of God.

Billy Graham

Get rich quick! Count your blessings!

Anonymous

Only through routine, regular exposure to God's Word can you and I draw out the nutrition needed to grow a heart of faith.

Elizabeth George

MORE FROM GOD'S WORD

As for you, if you walk before Me as your father David walked, with integrity of heart and uprightness, doing everything I have commanded you, and if you keep My statutes and ordinances, I will establish your royal throne over Israel forever, as I promised your father David.

1 Kings 9:4-5 HCSB

Come to terms with God and be at peace; in this way good will come to you.

Job 22:21 HCSB

The Lord bless you and protect you; the Lord make His face shine on you, and be gracious to you.

Numbers 6:24-25 HCSB

Blessed is a man who endures trials, because when he passes the test he will receive the crown of life that He has promised to those who love Him.

James 1:12 HCSB

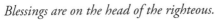

Blessings are on the head of the righteous.

Proverbs 10:6 HCSB

Those who are blessed by Him will inherit the land.

Psalm 37:22 HCSB

Let not your heart be troubled: ye believe in God, believe also in me. In my Father's house are many mansions: if it were not so, I would have told you. I go to prepare a place for you. And if I go and prepare a place for you, I will come again, and receive you unto myself; that where I am, there ye may be also.

John 14:1-3 KJV

Be glad and rejoice, because your reward is great in heaven.

Matthew 5:12 HCSB

A TIMELY TIP

God gives us countless blessings. We, in turn, should give Him our thanks and our praise.

COUNT YOUR BLESSINGS

In the space below, write down a few of the things you're most thankful for.

_____

_____

_____

_____

_____

_____

_____

_____

_____

_____

_____

_____

_____

_____

_____

CHAPTER 2

The Blessing of God's Love

Love consists in this: not that we loved God, but that He loved us and sent His Son to be the propitiation for our sins.

—1 John 4:10 HCSB

God's love for you is bigger and better than you can imagine. In fact, God's love is far too big to comprehend (in this lifetime). But this much we know: God loves you so much that He sent His Son Jesus to come to this earth and die for you. And, when you accepted Jesus into your heart, God gave you a gift that is more precious than gold: the gift of eternal life. Now, precisely because you are a wondrous creation treasured by God, a question presents itself: What will you do in response to God's love? Will you ignore it or embrace it? Will you return it or neglect it? The decision, of course, is yours and yours alone.

When you embrace God's love, you are forever changed. When you embrace God's love, you feel differently about yourself, your neighbors, and your world. When you embrace God's love, you share His message and you obey His commandments.

When you accept the Father's gift of grace, you are blessed here on earth and throughout all eternity. So do yourself a favor right now: accept God's love with open arms and welcome His Son Jesus into your heart. When you do, your life will be changed today, tomorrow, and forever.

Let God have you, and let God love you—and don't be surprised if your heart begins to hear music you've never heard and your feet learn to dance as never before.

—

Max Lucado

MORE IMPORTANT IDEAS ABOUT GOD'S LOVE

The question of whether or not God loves you and is concerned about you has nothing to do with the circumstances surrounding you right now. That question was settled a long time ago.

Charles Stanley

To lose us was too great a pain for God to bear, and so he took it upon himself to rescue us. The Son of God came "to give his life as a ransom for many" (Matt. 20:28).

John Eldredge

Life in God is a great big hug that lasts forever!

Barbara Johnson

When God tells us to love our enemies, he gives, along with the command, the love itself.

Corrie ten Boom

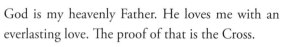

God is my heavenly Father. He loves me with an everlasting love. The proof of that is the Cross.

Elisabeth Elliot

The hope we have in Jesus is the anchor for the soul—something sure and steadfast, preventing drifting or giving way, lowered to the depth of God's love.

Franklin Graham

God's love did not begin at Calvary. Before the world was baptized with the first light, before the first blades of tender grass peeped out, God was love.

Billy Graham

Joy comes from knowing God loves me and knows who I am and where I'm going . . . that my future is secure as I rest in Him.

James Dobson

MORE FROM GOD'S WORD

We love Him because He first loved us.

1 John 4:19 NKJV

Draw near to God, and He will draw near to you.

James 4:8 HCSB

For He is gracious and compassionate, slow to anger, rich in faithful love.

Joel 2:13 HCSB

For God loved the world in this way: He gave His only Son, so that everyone who believes in Him will not perish but have eternal life.

John 3:16 HCSB

A TIMELY TIP

God's love for you is too big to understand, but it's not too big to share.

COUNT YOUR BLESSINGS

In the space below, write down your thoughts about God's love.

_____

_____

_____

_____

_____

_____

_____

_____

_____

_____

_____

_____

_____

_____

_____

CHAPTER 3

The Blessing of God's Abundance

I have come that they may have life, and that they may have it more abundantly.

—John 10:10 NKJV

God offers us abundance through His Son Jesus. Whether or not we accept God's abundance is, of course, up to each of us. When we entrust our hearts and our days to the One who created us, we experience abundance through the grace and sacrifice of His Son Jesus. But, when we turn our thoughts and our energies away from God's commandments, we inevitably forfeit the spiritual abundance that might otherwise be ours.

What is your focus today? Are you focused on God's Word and His will for your life? Or are you focused on the distractions and temptations of a difficult world? The answer to this question will, to a surprising extent, determine the quality and the direction of your day.

If you sincerely seek the spiritual abundance that your Savior offers, then follow Him completely and without reservation. When you do, you will receive the love, the life, and the abundance that He has promised.

The gift of God is eternal life,
spiritual life, abundant life
through faith in Jesus Christ,
the Living Word of God.

—

Anne Graham Lotz

MORE IMPORTANT IDEAS ABOUT GOD'S ABUNDANCE

The only way you can experience abundant life is to surrender your plans to Him.

Charles Stanley

Instead of living a black-and-white existence, we'll be released into a Technicolor world of vibrancy and emotion when we more accurately reflect His nature to the world around us.

Bill Hybels

God's riches are beyond anything we could ask or even dare to imagine! If my life gets gooey and stale, I have no excuse.

Barbara Johnson

Yes, we were created for His holy pleasure, but we will ultimately—if not immediately—find much pleasure in His pleasure.

Beth Moore

Jesus intended for us to be overwhelmed by the blessings of regular days. He said it was the reason he had come: "I am come that they might have life, and that they might have it more abundantly."

Gloria Gaither

God loves you and wants you to experience peace and life—abundant and eternal.

Billy Graham

God is the giver, and we are the receivers. And His richest gifts are bestowed not upon those who do the greatest things, but upon those who accept His abundance and His grace.

Hannah Whitall Smith

God has promised us abundance, peace, and eternal life. These treasures are ours for the asking; all we must do is claim them. One of the great mysteries of life is why on earth do so many of us wait so very long to lay claim to God's gifts?

Marie T. Freeman

MORE FROM GOD'S WORD

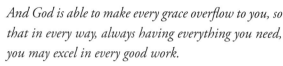

And God is able to make every grace overflow to you, so that in every way, always having everything you need, you may excel in every good work.

2 Corinthians 9:8 HCSB

I am the Alpha and the Omega, the Beginning and the End. I will give to the thirsty from the spring of living water as a gift.

Revelation 21:6 HCSB

It is good to give thanks to the Lord, to sing praises to the Most High. It is good to proclaim your unfailing love in the morning, your faithfulness in the evening.

Psalm 92:1-2 NLT

A TIMELY TIP

God wants to shower you with abundance—your job is to let Him.

COUNT YOUR BLESSINGS

In the space below, write down your thoughts about God's abundance.

_____

_____

_____

_____

_____

_____

_____

_____

_____

_____

_____

_____

_____

_____

_____

_____

CHAPTER 4

The Blessing of God's Peace

And the peace of God, which surpasses every thought, will guard your hearts and your minds in Christ Jesus. Finally brothers, whatever is true, whatever is honorable, whatever is just, whatever is pure, whatever is lovely, whatever is commendable—if there is any moral excellence and if there is any praise—dwell on these things.

—Philippians 4:7-8 HCSB

Are you at peace with the direction of your life? Or are you still rushing after the illusion of "peace and happiness" that our world promises but cannot deliver? The answer to this simple question will determine, to a surprising extent, the direction and the quality of your day and your life.

Joyce Meyer observes, "We need to be at peace with our past, content with our present, and sure about our future, knowing they are all in God's hands."

Today, as a gift to yourself, to your family, and to your friends, claim the inner peace that is your spiritual birthright. It is offered freely; it is yours for the asking. So ask. And then share.

I believe that in every time and
place it is within our power
to acquiesce in the will of God—
and what peace it brings to do so!

—

Elisabeth Elliot

MORE IMPORTANT IDEAS ABOUT FINDING PEACE

To know God as He really is—in His essential nature and character—is to arrive at a citadel of peace that circumstances may storm, but can never capture.

Catherine Marshall

That peace, which has been described and which believers enjoy, is a participation of the peace which their glorious Lord and Master himself enjoys.

Jonathan Edwards

The fruit of our placing all things in God's hands is the presence of His abiding peace in our hearts.

Hannah Whitall Smith

There may be no trumpet sound or loud applause when we make a right decision, just a calm sense of resolution and peace.

Gloria Gaither

A great many people are trying to make peace, but that has already been done. God has not left it for us to do; all we have to do is to enter into it.

D. L. Moody

Prayer guards hearts and minds and causes God to bring peace out of chaos.

Beth Moore

Peace with God is where all peace begins.

Jim Gallery

When we do what is right, we have contentment, peace, and happiness.

Beverly LaHaye

In the center of a hurricane there is absolute quiet and peace. There is no safer place than in the center of the will of God.

Corrie ten Boom

MORE FROM GOD'S WORD

So then, we must pursue what promotes peace and what builds up one another.

Romans 14:19 HCSB

If possible, on your part, live at peace with everyone.

Romans 12:18 HCSB

For the mind-set of the flesh is death, but the mind-set of the Spirit is life and peace.

Romans 8:6 HCSB

Blessed are the peacemakers, for they shall be called sons of God.

Matthew 5:9 NKJV

A TIMELY TIP

God offers peace that passes human understanding . . . and He wants you to make His peace your peace.

COUNT YOUR BLESSINGS

In the space below, write down your thoughts about things you can do to find—and keep—God's peace in your heart.

_____

_____

_____

_____

_____

_____

_____

_____

_____

_____

_____

_____

_____

CHAPTER 5

The Blessing of Family

Choose for yourselves today the one you will worship . . . . As for me and my family, we will worship the Lord.

—Joshua 24:15 HCSB

These are difficult days for our nation and for our families. But, thankfully, God is bigger than all of our challenges. God loves us and protects us. In times of trouble, He comforts us; in times of sorrow, He dries our tears. When we are troubled, or weak, or sorrowful, God is as near as our next breath.

Are you concerned for the well-being of your family? You are not alone. We live in a world where temptation and danger seem to lurk on every street corner. Parents and children alike have good reason to be watchful. But, despite the evils of our time, God remains steadfast. Let us build our lives on the rock that cannot be shaken . . . let us trust in our Creator. Even in these difficult days, no problem is too big for God.

MORE IMPORTANT IDEAS ABOUT THE BLESSING OF FAMILY

The only true source of meaning in life is found in love for God and his son Jesus Christ, and love for mankind, beginning with our own families.

James Dobson

Calm and peaceful, the home should be the one place where people are certain they will be welcomed, received, protected, and loved.

Ed Young

A family is a place where principles are hammered and honed on the anvil of everyday living.

Charles Swindoll

A home is a place where we find direction.

Gigi Graham Tchividjian

The Golden Rule begins at home.

Marie T. Freeman

The miraculous thing about
being a family is that in the last
analysis, we are each dependent of
one another and God,
woven together by mercy given
and mercy received.

—

Barbara Johnson

MORE FROM GOD'S WORD

If a kingdom is divided against itself, that kingdom cannot stand. If a house is divided against itself, that house cannot stand.

Mark 3:24-25 HCSB

The one who brings ruin on his household will inherit the wind.

Proverbs 11:29 HCSB

Unless the Lord builds a house, its builders labor over it in vain; unless the Lord watches over a city, the watchman stays alert in vain.

Psalm 127:1 HCSB

Love must be without hypocrisy. Detest evil; cling to what is good. Show family affection to one another with brotherly love. Outdo one another in showing honor.

Romans 12:9-10 HCSB

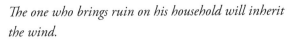

The one who brings ruin on his household will inherit the wind.

Proverbs 11:29 HCSB

You must get along with each other. You must learn to be considerate of one another, cultivating a life in common.

1 Corinthians 1:10 MSG

Don't you realize that all of you together are the temple of God and that the Spirit of God lives in you?

1 Corinthians 3:16 NLT

How good and pleasant it is when brothers can live together!

Psalm 133:1 HCSB

A TIMELY TIP

Your family is a precious gift from above, a gift that should be treasured, nurtured, and loved.

COUNT YOUR BLESSINGS

In the space below, write down your thoughts about the blessing of family.

_____

_____

_____

_____

_____

_____

_____

_____

_____

_____

_____

_____

CHAPTER 6

Count Your Blessings and Guard Your Thoughts

As for you, Solomon my son, know the God of your father, and serve Him with a whole heart and a willing mind, for the Lord searches every heart and understands the intention of every thought. If you seek Him, He will be found by you, but if you forsake Him, He will reject you forever.

—1 Chronicles 28:9 HCSB

Because we are human, we are always busy with our thoughts. We simply can't help ourselves. Our brains never shut off, and even while we're sleeping, we mull things over in our minds. The question is not if we will think; the question is how will we think and what will we think about.

Today, focus your thoughts on God and His will. And if you've been plagued by pessimism and doubt, stop thinking like that! Place your faith in

God and give thanks for His blessings. Think optimistically about your world and your life. It's the wise way to use your mind. And besides, since you will always be busy with your thoughts, you might as well make those thoughts pleasing (to God) and helpful (to you and yours).

The things we think are the things that feed our souls. If we think on pure and lovely things, we shall grow pure and lovely like them; and the converse is equally true.

—

Hannah Whitall Smith

MORE IMPORTANT IDEAS ABOUT YOUR THOUGHTS AND YOUR LIFE

It is the thoughts and intents of the heart that shape a person's life.

John Eldredge

I need the spiritual revival that comes from spending quiet time alone with Jesus in prayer and in thoughtful meditation on His Word.

Anne Graham Lotz

No matter how little we can change about our circumstances, we always have a choice about our attitude toward the situation.

Vonette Bright

Whether we think of, or speak to, God, whether we act or suffer for him, all is prayer when we have no other object than his love and the desire of pleasing him.

John Wesley

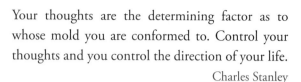

Your thoughts are the determining factor as to whose mold you are conformed to. Control your thoughts and you control the direction of your life.

Charles Stanley

People who do not develop and practice good thinking often find themselves at the mercy of their circumstances.

John Maxwell

As we have by faith said no to sin, so we should by faith say yes to God and set our minds on things above, where Christ is seated in the heavenlies.

Vonette Bright

No more imperfect thoughts. No more sad memories. No more ignorance. My redeemed body will have a redeemed mind. Grant me a foretaste of that perfect mind as you mirror your thoughts in me today.

Joni Eareckson Tada

MORE FROM GOD'S WORD

Brothers, don't be childish in your thinking, but be infants in evil and adult in your thinking.

1 Corinthians 14:20 HCSB

Set your minds on what is above, not on what is on the earth.

Colossians 3:2 HCSB

I, the Lord, examine the mind, I test the heart to give to each according to his way, according to what his actions deserve.

Jeremiah 17:10 HCSB

A TIMELY TIP

Your thoughts have the power to lift you up or bring you down, so you should guard your thoughts very carefully. Either you control your thoughts, or they most certainly will control you.

COUNT YOUR BLESSINGS

In the space below, write down a few of the simple blessings that God is giving you today.

_____

_____

_____

_____

_____

_____

_____

_____

_____

_____

_____

_____

_____

_____

_____

CHAPTER 7

The Blessing of Laughter

There is an occasion for everything, and a time for every activity under heaven . . . a time to weep and a time to laugh; a time to mourn and a time to dance.

—Ecclesiastes 3:1, 4 HCSB

Laughter is a gift from God, a gift that He intends for us to use. Yet sometimes, because of the inevitable stresses of everyday living, we fail to find the fun in life. When we allow life's inevitable disappointments to cast a pall over our lives and our souls, we do a profound disservice to ourselves and to our loved ones.

If you've allowed the clouds of life to obscure the blessings of life, perhaps you've formed the unfortunate habit of taking things just a little too seriously. If so, it's time to fret a little less and laugh a little more.

So today, look for the humor that most certainly surrounds you—when you do, you'll find it. And remember: God created laughter for a reason . . . and Father indeed knows best. So laugh!

MORE IMPORTANT IDEAS ABOUT
THE BLESSING OF LAUGHTER

When we bring sunshine into the lives of others, we're warmed by it ourselves. When we spill a little happiness, it splashes on us.

Barbara Johnson

We may run, walk, stumble, drive, or fly, but let us never lose sight of the reason for the journey, or miss a chance to see a rainbow on the way.

Gloria Gaither

The people whom I have seen succeed best in life have always been cheerful and hopeful people who went about their business with a smile on their faces.

Charles Kingsley

Christ can put a spring in your step and a thrill in your heart. Optimism and cheerfulness are products of knowing Christ.

Billy Graham

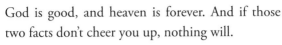

God is good, and heaven is forever. And if those two facts don't cheer you up, nothing will.

Marie T. Freeman

If you want people to feel comfortable around you, to enjoy being with you, then learn to laugh at yourself and find humor in life's little mishaps.

Dennis Swanberg

He who laughs lasts—he who doesn't, doesn't.

Marie T. Freeman

I think everybody ought to be a laughing Christian. I'm convinced that there's just one place where there's not any laughter, and that's hell.

Jerry Clower

Laughter is to life what shock absorbers are to automobiles. It won't take the potholes out of the road, but it sure makes the ride smoother.

Barbara Johnson

MORE FROM GOD'S WORD

A joyful heart makes a face cheerful.

Proverbs 15:13 HCSB

Oh, clap your hands, all you peoples! Shout to God with the voice of triumph!

Psalm 47:1 NKJV

And not only so, but we also joy in God through our Lord Jesus Christ, by whom we have now received the atonement.

Romans 5:11 KJV

The Lord reigns; let the earth rejoice.

Psalm 97:1 NKJV

I will thank the Lord with all my heart; I will declare all Your wonderful works. I will rejoice and boast about You; I will sing about Your name, Most High.

Psalm 9:1-2 HCSB

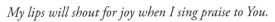

My lips will shout for joy when I sing praise to You.

Psalm 71:23 HCSB

Make me hear joy and gladness.

Psalm 51:8 NKJV

My cup runs over. Surely goodness and mercy shall follow me all the days of my life; and I will dwell in the house of the Lord Forever.

Psalm 23:5-6 NKJV

Be cheerful no matter what; pray all the time; thank God no matter what happens. This is the way God wants you who belong to Christ Jesus to live.

1 Thessalonians 5:16-18 MSG

A TIMELY TIP

Learn to laugh at life. Life has a lighter side—look for it, especially when times are tough. Laughter is medicine for the soul, so take your medicine early and often.

COUNT YOUR BLESSINGS

In the space below, write down your thoughts about the joys of laughter.

_____

_____

_____

_____

_____

_____

_____

_____

_____

_____

_____

_____

_____

CHAPTER 8

A Simple Blessing for the World: Your Smile

Happy are the people whose strength is in You, whose hearts are set on pilgrimage.

—Psalm 84:5 HCSB

A smile is nourishment for the heart, and laughter is medicine for the soul—but sometimes, amid the stresses of the day, we forget to take our medicine. Instead of viewing our world with a mixture of optimism and humor, we allow worries and distractions to rob us of the joy that God intends for our lives.

So the next time you find yourself dwelling upon the negatives of life, refocus your attention on things positive. The next time you find yourself falling prey to the blight of pessimism, stop yourself and turn your thoughts around. With a loving God as your protector, and with a loving family to support you, you're blessed now and forever.

So smile . . . starting now!

A smile is the light
in the window of your face that
tells people you're at home.

—

Barbara Johnson

MORE IMPORTANT IDEAS ABOUT HAPPINESS

When the dream of our heart is one that God has planted there, a strange happiness flows into us. At that moment, all of the spiritual resources of the universe are released to help us. Our praying is then at one with the will of God and becomes a channel for the Creator's purposes for us and our world.

Catherine Marshall

Our thoughts, not our circumstances, determine our happiness.

John Maxwell

Life goes on. Keep on smiling and the whole world smiles with you.

Dennis Swanberg

The happiest people in the world are not those who have no problems, but the people who have learned to live with those things that are less than perfect.

James Dobson

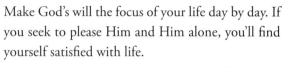

Make God's will the focus of your life day by day. If you seek to please Him and Him alone, you'll find yourself satisfied with life.

Kay Arthur

We will never be happy until we make God the source of our fulfillment and the answer to our longings.

Stormie Omartian

A smile is a curve that helps set things straight.

Anonymous

When we do what is right, we have contentment, peace, and happiness.

Beverly LaHaye

I am truly happy with Jesus Christ. I couldn't live without Him.

Ruth Bell Graham

MORE FROM GOD'S WORD

Happy is the one whose help is the God of Jacob, whose hope is in the Lord his God.

Psalm 146:5 HCSB

How happy is everyone who fears the Lord, who walks in His ways!

Psalm 128:1 HCSB

How happy are those whose way is blameless, who live according to the law of the Lord! Happy are those who keep His decrees and seek Him with all their heart.

Psalm 119:1-2 HCSB

A TIMELY TIP

Today, make it a point to smile as much as you can. It's good for your health, and it makes those around you feel better, too.

COUNT YOUR BLESSINGS

In the space below, write down your thoughts about some of the simple blessings that make you happy.

_____

_____

_____

_____

_____

_____

_____

_____

_____

_____

_____

_____

_____

_____

CHAPTER 9

The Blessing of Love

Now these three remain: faith, hope, and love. But the greatest of these is love.

—1 Corinthians 13:13 HCSB

Love, like everything else in this wonderful world, begins and ends with God, but the middle part belongs to us. During the brief time that we have here on earth, God has given each of us the opportunity to become a loving person—or not. God has given each of us the opportunity to be kind, to be courteous, to be cooperative, and to be forgiving—or not. God has given each of us the chance to obey the Golden Rule, or to make up our own rules as we go. If we obey God's rules, we're safe, but if we do otherwise, we're headed for trouble and fast.

Here in the real world, the choices that we make have consequences. The decisions that we make and the results of those decisions determine the quality of our relationships. It's as simple as that.

If Jesus is the preeminent One
in our lives, then we will love
each other, submit to each other,
and treat one another
fairly in the Lord.

—

Warren Wiersbe

MORE IMPORTANT IDEAS ABOUT LOVE

To have fallen in love hints to our hearts that all of earthly life is not hopelessly fallen. Love is the laughter of God.

Beth Moore

Those who abandon ship the first time it enters a storm miss the calm beyond. And the rougher the storms weathered together, the deeper and stronger real love grows.

Ruth Bell Graham

Love is an attribute of God. To love others is evidence of a genuine faith.

Kay Arthur

Live your lives in love, the same sort of love which Christ gives us, and which He perfectly expressed when He gave Himself as a sacrifice to God.

Corrie ten Boom

How do you spell love? When you reach the point where the happiness, security, and development of another person is as much of a driving force to you as your own happiness, security, and development, then you have a mature love. True love is spelled G-I-V-E. It is not based on what you can get, but rooted in what you can give to the other person.

Josh McDowell

Love must be supported and fed and protected, just like a little infant who is growing up at home.

James Dobson

Love is the seed of all hope. It is the enticement to trust, to risk, to try, and to go on.

Gloria Gaither

It is when we come to the Lord in our nothingness, our powerlessness and our helplessness that He then enables us to love in a way which, without Him, would be absolutely impossible.

Elisabeth Elliot

MORE FROM GOD'S WORD

The one who loves his brother remains in the light, and there is no cause for stumbling in him.

1 John 2:10 HCSB

Dear friends, if God loved us in this way, we also must love one another.

1 John 4:11 HCSB

Love one another earnestly from a pure heart.

1 Peter 1:22 HCSB

Above all, keep your love for one another at full strength, since love covers a multitude of sins.

1 Peter 4:8 HCSB

A TIMELY TIP

There are many ways to say, "I love you." Find them. Use them. And keep using them.

COUNT YOUR BLESSINGS

In the space below, write down your thoughts about the loved ones God has placed along your path.

CHAPTER 10

Keep Growing!

Therefore, leaving the elementary message about the Messiah, let us go on to maturity.

—Hebrews 6:1 HCSB

Are you continuing to grow in your love and knowledge of the Lord, or are you "satisfied" with the current state of your spiritual health? Your relationship with God is ongoing; it unfolds day by day, and it offers countless opportunities to grow closer to Him . . . or not. As each new day unfolds, you are confronted with a wide range of decisions: how you will behave, where you will direct your thoughts, with whom you will associate, and what you will choose to worship. These choices, along with many others like them, are yours and yours alone. How you choose determines how your relationship with God will unfold.

Hopefully, you're determined to make yourself a growing Christian. Your Savior deserves no less, and neither, by the way, do you.

MORE IMPORTANT IDEAS ABOUT SPIRITUAL GROWTH

God is teaching me to become more and more "teachable": To keep evolving. To keep taking the risk of learning something new . . . or unlearning something old and off base.

Beth Moore

Our vision is so limited we can hardly imagine a love that does not show itself in protection from suffering. The love of God did not protect His own Son. He will not necessarily protect us—not from anything it takes to make us like His Son. A lot of hammering and chiseling and purifying by fire will have to go into the process.

Elisabeth Elliot

Growth takes place in quietness, in hidden ways, in silence and solitude. The process is not accessible to observation.

Eugene Peterson

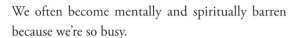

We often become mentally and spiritually barren because we're so busy.

Franklin Graham

Be filled with the Holy Spirit; join a church where the members believe the Bible and know the Lord; seek the fellowship of other Christians; learn and be nourished by God's Word and His many promises. Conversion is not the end of your journey—it is only the beginning.

Corrie ten Boom

I'm not what I want to be. I'm not what I'm going to be. But, thank God, I'm not what I was!

Gloria Gaither

Grow, dear friends, but grow, I beseech you, in God's way, which is the only true way.

Hannah Whitall Smith

Salvation is not an event; it is a process.

Henry Blackaby

MORE FROM GOD'S WORD

For You, O God, have tested us; You have refined us as silver is refined. You brought us into the net; You laid affliction on our backs. You have caused men to ride over our heads; we went through fire and through water; but You brought us out to rich fulfillment.

Psalm 66:10-12 NKJV

Leave inexperience behind, and you will live; pursue the way of understanding.

Proverbs 9:6 HCSB

I want their hearts to be encouraged and joined together in love, so that they may have all the riches of assured understanding, and have the knowledge of God's mystery—Christ.

Colossians 2:2 HCSB

For this reason also, since the day we heard this, we haven't stopped praying for you. We are asking that you may be filled with the knowledge of His will in all wisdom and spiritual understanding.

Colossians 1:9 HCSB

But the man who looks intently into the perfect law that gives freedom, and continues to do this, not forgetting what he has heard, but doing it—he will be blessed in what he does.

James 1:25 NIV

But grow in the grace and knowledge of our Lord and Savior Jesus Christ. To Him be the glory both now and to the day of eternity.

2 Peter 3:18 HCSB

The Lord says, "I will guide you along the best pathway for your life. I will advise you and watch over you."

Psalm 32:8 NLT

A THOUGHT TO REMEMBER

When it comes to walking with God, there is no such thing as instant maturity. God doesn't mass produce His saints. He hand tools each one, and it always takes longer than we expected.

Charles Swindoll

COUNT YOUR BLESSINGS

In the space below, write down your thoughts about the rewards that can be yours when you continue to grow spiritually and emotionally.

_____

_____

_____

_____

_____

_____

_____

_____

_____

_____

_____

_____

_____

_____

CHAPTER 11

The Blessing of Prayer

The intense prayer of the righteous is very powerful.
—James 5:16 HCSB

Prayer is a priceless blessing and a powerful tool for communicating with our Creator; it is an opportunity to commune with the Giver of all things good. Prayer is not a thing to be taken lightly or to be used infrequently. Prayer should never be reserved for mealtimes or for bedtimes; it should be an ever-present focus in our daily lives.

In his first letter to the Thessalonians, Paul wrote, "Rejoice evermore. Pray without ceasing. In every thing give thanks: for this is the will of God in Christ Jesus concerning you" (5:17-18 KJV). Paul's words apply to every Christian of every generation.

Instead of turning things over in our minds, let us turn them over to God in prayer. Instead of worrying about our decisions, let's trust God to help us make them. Today, let us pray constantly about things great and small. God is listening, and He wants to hear from us. Now.

MORE IMPORTANT IDEAS ABOUT PRAYER

A life growing in its purity and devotion will be a more prayerful life.

E. M. Bounds

God knows that we, with our limited vision, don't even know that for which we should pray. When we entrust our requests to him, we trust him to honor our prayers with holy judgment.

Max Lucado

Prayer guards hearts and minds and causes God to bring peace out of chaos.

Beth Moore

Find a place to pray where no one imagines that you are praying. Then, shut the door and talk to God.

Oswald Chambers

Prayer connects us with God's limitless potential.

Henry Blackaby

To pray is to mount on eagle's wings above the clouds and get into the clear heaven where God dwells.

C. H. Spurgeon

We forget that God sometimes has to say "No." We pray to Him as our heavenly Father, and like wise human fathers, He often says, "No," not from whim or caprice, but from wisdom, from love, and from knowing what is best for us.

Peter Marshall

When we pray, the first thing we should do is to see to it that we really get an audience with God, that we really get into His very presence. Before a word of petition is offered, we should have the definite consciousness that we are talking to God, and we should believe that He is listening.

R. A. Torrey

MORE FROM GOD'S WORD

Let the words of my mouth and the meditation of my heart be acceptable in Your sight, O Lord, my strength and my Redeemer.

Psalm 19:14 NKJV

Yet He often withdrew to deserted places and prayed.

Luke 5:16 HCSB

Don't worry about anything, but in everything, through prayer and petition with thanksgiving, let your requests be made known to God.

Philippians 4:6 HCSB

And in that day you will ask Me nothing. Most assuredly, I say to you, whatever you ask the Father in My name He will give you. Until now you have asked nothing in My name. Ask, and you will receive, that your joy may be full.

John 16:23-24 NKJV

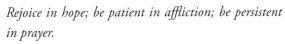

Rejoice in hope; be patient in affliction; be persistent in prayer.

Romans 12:12 HCSB

Rejoice always! Pray constantly. Give thanks in everything, for this is God's will for you in Christ Jesus.

1 Thessalonians 5:16-18 HCSB

Ask and it shall be given to you; seek and you shall find; knock and it shall be opened to you. For every one who asks receives, and he who seeks finds, and to him who knocks it shall be opened.

Matthew 7:7-8 NASB

A THOUGHT TO REMEMBER

Wasted time of which we are later ashamed, temptations we yield to, weaknesses, lethargy in our work, disorder and lack of discipline in our thoughts and in our interaction with others—all these frequently have their root in neglecting prayer in the morning.

Dietrich Bonhoeffer

COUNT YOUR BLESSINGS

In the space below, write down your thoughts about the importance of prayer.

_____

_____

_____

_____

_____

_____

_____

_____

_____

_____

_____

_____

_____

_____

_____

CHAPTER 12

The Blessing of Hope

But if we hope for what we do not see, we eagerly wait for it with patience.

—Romans 8:25 HCSB

The hope that the world offers is fleeting and imperfect. The hope that God offers is unchanging, unshakable, and unending. It is no wonder, then, that when we seek security from worldly sources, our hopes are often dashed. Thankfully, God has no such record of failure.

Where will you place your hopes today? Will you entrust your future to man or to God? Will you seek solace exclusively from fallible human beings, or will you place your hopes, first and foremost, in the trusting hands of your Creator? The decision is yours, and you must live with the results of the choice you make.

For thoughtful believers, hope begins with God. Period. So today, as you embark upon the next stage of your life's journey, consider the words of the Psalmist: "You are my hope; O Lord GOD,

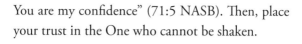

You are my confidence" (71:5 NASB). Then, place your trust in the One who cannot be shaken.

MORE IMPORTANT IDEAS ABOUT HOPE

The best we can hope for in this life is a knothole peek at the shining realities ahead. Yet a glimpse is enough. It's enough to convince our hearts that whatever sufferings and sorrows currently assail us aren't worthy of comparison to that which waits over the horizon.

Joni Eareckson Tada

Faith looks back and draws courage; hope looks ahead and keeps desire alive.

John Eldredge

I discovered that sorrow was not to be feared but rather endured with hope and expectancy that God would use it to visit and bless my life.

Jill Briscoe

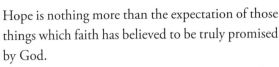

Hope is nothing more than the expectation of those things which faith has believed to be truly promised by God.

John Calvin

Oh, remember this: There is never a time when we may not hope in God. Whatever our necessities, however great our difficulties, and though to all appearance help is impossible, yet our business is to hope in God, and it will be found that it is not in vain.

George Mueller

Love is the seed of all hope. It is the enticement to trust, to risk, to try, and to go on.

Gloria Gaither

Hope looks for the good in people, opens doors for people, discovers what can be done to help, lights a candle, does not yield to cynicism. Hope sets people free.

Barbara Johnson

MORE FROM GOD'S WORD

We have this hope—like a sure and firm anchor of the soul—that enters the inner sanctuary behind the curtain.

Hebrews 6:19 HCSB

I assure you: The one who believes in Me will also do the works that I do. And he will do even greater works than these, because I am going to the Father.

John 14:12 HCSB

Therefore we do not lose heart. Even though our outward man is perishing, yet the inward man is being renewed day by day.

2 Corinthians 4:16 NKJV

Looking at them, Jesus said, "With men it is impossible, but not with God, because all things are possible with God."

Mark 10:27 HCSB

But as it is written: "Eye has not seen, nor ear heard, nor have entered into the heart of man the things which God has prepared for those who love Him."

1 Corinthians 2:9 NKJV

But I will hope continually and will praise You more and more.

Psalm 71:14 HCSB

Rejoice in hope; be patient in affliction; be persistent in prayer.

Romans 12:12 HCSB

Let us hold on to the confession of our hope without wavering, for He who promised is faithful.

Hebrews 10:23 HCSB

A TIMELY TIP

Never be afraid to hope—or to ask—for a miracle.

COUNT YOUR BLESSINGS

In the space below, write down some of the things you're hopeful for.

_____

_____

_____

_____

_____

_____

_____

_____

_____

_____

_____

_____

_____

_____

CHAPTER 13

The Blessing of Forgiveness

And be kind to one another, tenderhearted, forgiving one another, just as God in Christ forgave you.
—Ephesians 4:32 NKJV

How often must we forgive family members and friends? More times than we can count. Our children are precious but imperfect; so are our spouses and our friends. We must, on occasion, forgive those who have injured us; to do otherwise is to disobey God.

Are you easily frustrated by the inevitable imperfections of others? Are you a prisoner of bitterness and regret? If so, perhaps you need a refresher course in the art of forgiveness.

If there exists even one person, alive or dead, whom you have not forgiven (including yourself), follow God's commandment and His will for your life: forgive. Bitterness, anger, and regret are not part of God's plan for your life. Forgiveness is.

MORE IMPORTANT IDEAS ABOUT THE GIFT OF FORGIVENESS

The fact is, God no longer deals with us in judgment but in mercy. If people got what they deserved, this old planet would have ripped apart at the seams centuries ago. Praise God that because of His great love "we are not consumed, for his compassions never fail" (Lam. 3:22).

Joni Eareckson Tada

When God forgives, He forgets. He buries our sins in the sea and puts a sign on the shore saying, "No Fishing Allowed."

Corrie ten Boom

The more you practice the art of forgiving, the quicker you'll master the art of living.

Marie T. Freeman

It is better to forgive and forget than to resent and remember.

Barbara Johnson

Forgiveness is the precondition of love.

Catherine Marshall

To hold on to hate and resentments is to throw a monkey wrench into the machinery of life.

E. Stanley Jones

I firmly believe a great many prayers are not answered because we are not willing to forgive someone.

D. L. Moody

Our relationships with other people are of primary importance to God. Because God is love, He cannot tolerate any unforgiveness or hardness in us toward any individual.

Catherine Marshall

Forgiveness is not an emotion. Forgiveness is an act of the will, and the will can function regardless of the temperature of the heart.

Corrie ten Boom

MORE FROM GOD'S WORD

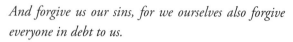

And forgive us our sins, for we ourselves also forgive everyone in debt to us.

Luke 11:4 HCSB

The one who blesses others is abundantly blessed; those who help others are helped.

Proverbs 11:25 MSG

Then Jesus said, "Father, forgive them, for they do not know what they do." And they divided His garments and cast lots.

Luke 23:34 NKJV

A person's insight gives him patience, and his virtue is to overlook an offense.

Proverbs 19:11 HCSB

Lord, You are my lamp; the Lord illuminates my darkness.

2 Samuel 22:29 HCSB

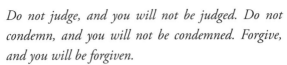

Do not judge, and you will not be judged. Do not condemn, and you will not be condemned. Forgive, and you will be forgiven.

Luke 6:37 HCSB

When we have the opportunity to help anyone, we should do it. But we should give special attention to those who are in the family of believers.

Galatians 6:10 NCV

Then Peter came to Him and said, "Lord, how many times could my brother sin against me and I forgive him? As many as seven times?" "I tell you, not as many as seven," Jesus said to him, "but 70 times seven."

Matthew 18:21-22 HCSB

A TIMELY TIP

Forgiveness is its own reward. Bitterness is its own punishment. Guard your words and your thoughts accordingly.

COUNT YOUR BLESSINGS

In the space below, write down your thoughts about the blessings that can be yours when you forgive.

CHAPTER 14

Count Your Blessings and Praise the Lord

Sing to the Lord, all the earth; Proclaim the good news of His salvation from day to day.

—1 Chronicles 16:23 NKJV

The words by Fanny Crosby are familiar: "This is my story, this is my song, praising my Savior, all the day long." And, as believers who have been saved by the blood of a risen Christ, we must do exactly as the song instructs: we must praise our Savior many times each day.

Worship and praise must be woven into the fabric of everything we do. Otherwise, we quickly lose perspective as we fall prey to the demands of everyday life.

Do you sincerely seek to be a worthy servant of the One who has given you eternal love and eternal life? Then praise Him for who He is and for what He has done for you. And don't just praise Him on Sunday morning. Praise Him all day long,

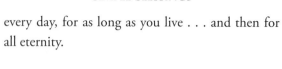

every day, for as long as you live . . . and then for all eternity.

MORE IMPORTANT IDEAS ABOUT PRAISE

Praise is the sparkplug of faith. Praise gets faith airborne where it can soar above the gravitational forces of this world's cares.

Kay Arthur

Preoccupy my thoughts with your praise beginning today.

Joni Eareckson Tada

God is worthy of our praise and is pleased when we come before Him with thanksgiving.

Shirley Dobson

This is my story, this is my song, praising my Savior, all the day long.

Fanny Crosby

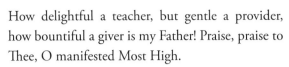

How delightful a teacher, but gentle a provider, how bountiful a giver is my Father! Praise, praise to Thee, O manifested Most High.

Jim Elliot

Worship is an act which develops feelings for God, not a feeling for God which is expressed in an act of worship. When we obey the command to praise God in worship, our deep, essential need to be in relationship with God is nurtured.

Eugene Peterson

I am to praise God for all things, regardless of where they seem to originate. Doing this is the key to receiving the blessings of God. Praise will wash away my resentments.

Catherine Marshall

Praise reestablishes the proper chain of command; we recognize that the King is on the throne and that he has saved his people.

Max Lucado

MORE FROM GOD'S WORD

Therefore, through Him let us continually offer up to God a sacrifice of praise, that is, the fruit of our lips that confess His name.

Hebrews 13:15 HCSB

And suddenly there was with the angel a multitude of the heavenly host praising God and saying: "Glory to God in the highest, And on earth peace, goodwill toward men!"

Luke 2:13-14 NKJV

So that at the name of Jesus every knee should bow—of those who are in heaven and on earth and under the earth—and every tongue should confess that Jesus Christ is Lord, to the glory of God the Father.

Philippians 2:10-11 HCSB

And let the peace of the Messiah, to which you were also called in one body, control your hearts. Be thankful.

Colossians 3:15 HCSB

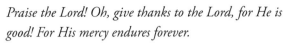

Praise the Lord! Oh, give thanks to the Lord, for He is good! For His mercy endures forever.

Psalm 106:1 NKJV

Thanks be to God for His indescribable gift.

2 Corinthians 9:15 HCSB

Give thanks to the Lord, for He is good; His faithful love endures forever.

Psalm 118:29 HCSB

In all your ways acknowledge Him, and He shall direct your paths.

Proverbs 3:6 NKJV

A TIMELY TIP

Remember that it always pays to praise your Creator. That's why it helps to carve out quiet moments throughout the day to praise God.

COUNT YOUR BLESSINGS

In the space below, write down your thoughts about
the need to praise God for your blessings.

_____

_____

_____

_____

_____

_____

_____

_____

_____

_____

_____

_____

_____

_____

_____

_____

CHAPTER 15

The Courage to Dream

Let us hold on to the confession of our hope without wavering, for He who promised is faithful.
—Hebrews 10:23 HCSB

It takes courage to dream big dreams. You will discover that courage when you do three things: accept the past, trust God to handle the future, and make the most of the time He has given you today.

Are you excited about the opportunities of today and thrilled by the possibilities of tomorrow? Do you confidently expect God to lead you to a place of abundance, peace, and joy? If you trust God's promises, you should believe that your future is intensely and eternally bright.

Today, promise yourself that you'll do the world a favor by whole-heartedly pursuing your dreams. After all, no dreams are too big for God—not even yours. So start living—and dreaming—accordingly.

Set goals so big that unless
God helps you, you will be
a miserable failure.

—

Bill Bright

MORE IMPORTANT IDEAS ABOUT YOUR DREAMS

Do not limit the limitless God! With Him, face the future unafraid because you are never alone.

Mrs. Charles E. Cowman

Allow your dreams a place in your prayers and plans. God-given dreams can help you move into the future He is preparing for you.

Barbara Johnson

To make your dream come true, you have to stay awake.

Dennis Swanberg

You cannot out-dream God.

John Eldredge

Determination and faithfulness are the nails used to build the house of God's dreams.

Barbara Johnson

MORE FROM GOD'S WORD

Where there is no vision, the people perish....

Proverbs 29:18 KJV

The Lord values those who fear Him, those who put their hope in His faithful love.

Psalm 147:11 HCSB

Lord, I turn my hope to You. My God, I trust in You.

Psalm 25:1-2 HCSB

But I will hope continually and will praise You more and more.

Psalm 71:14 HCSB

We have this hope—like a sure and firm anchor of the soul—that enters the inner sanctuary behind the curtain.

Hebrews 6:19 HCSB

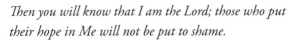

Then you will know that I am the Lord; those who put their hope in Me will not be put to shame.

Isaiah 49:23 HCSB

I wait for the Lord, my soul waits, and in His word I do hope. My soul waits for the Lord more than those who watch for the morning—Yes, more than those who watch for the morning.

Psalm 130:5-6 NKJV

A man's heart plans his way, but the Lord directs his steps.

Proverbs 16:9 NKJV

A THOUGHT TO REMEMBER

The future lies all before us. Shall it only be a slight advance upon what we usually do? Ought it not to be a bound, a leap forward to altitudes of endeavor and success undreamed of before?

Annie Armstrong

COUNT YOUR BLESSINGS

In the space below, write down your thoughts about the rewards that can be yours when you trust God and find the courage to follow your dreams.

_____

_____

_____

_____

_____

_____

_____

_____

_____

_____

_____

_____

_____

CHAPTER 16

The Simple Blessing of Encouragement

I want their hearts to be encouraged and joined together in love, so that they may have all the riches of assured understanding, and have the knowledge of God's mystery—Christ.

—Colossians 2:2 HCSB

L ife is a team sport, and all of us need occasional pats on the back from our teammates. As Christians, we are called upon to spread the Good News of Christ, and we are also called to spread a message of encouragement and hope to the world.

Whether you realize it or not, many people with whom you come in contact every day are in desperate need of a smile or an encouraging word. The world can be a difficult place, and countless friends and family members may be troubled by the challenges of everyday life. Since you don't always know who needs your help, the best strategy is to try to encourage all the people who cross your path. So today, be a world-class source of encouragement to everyone you meet. Never has the need been greater.

MORE IMPORTANT IDEAS ABOUT ENCOURAGEMENT

The balance of affirmation and discipline, freedom and restraint, encouragement and warning is different for each child and season and generation, yet the absolutes of God's Word are necessary and trustworthy at all times.

Gloria Gaither

Encouragement starts at home, but it should never end there.

Marie T. Freeman

God grant that we may not hinder those who are battling their way slowly into the light.

Oswald Chambers

I can usually sense that a leading is from the Holy Spirit when it calls me to humble myself, to serve somebody, to encourage somebody, or to give something away. Very rarely will the evil one lead us to do those kind of things.

Bill Hybels

God is still in the process of dispensing gifts, and He uses ordinary individuals like us to develop those gifts in other people.

Howard Hendricks

God of our life, there are days when the burdens we carry chafe our shoulders and weigh us down; when the road seems dreary and endless, the skies gray and threatening; when our lives have no music in them, and our hearts are lonely, and our souls have lost their courage. Flood the path with light, run our eyes to where the skies are full of promise; tune our hearts to brave music; give us the sense of comradeship with heroes and saints of every age; and so quicken our spirits that we may be able to encourage the souls of all who journey with us on the road of life, to Your honor and glory.

St. Augustine

MORE FROM GOD'S WORD

Carry one another's burdens; in this way you will fulfill the law of Christ.

Galatians 6:2 HCSB

But encourage each other daily, while it is still called today, so that none of you is hardened by sin's deception.

Hebrews 3:13 HCSB

And let us be concerned about one another in order to promote love and good works.

Hebrews 10:24 HCSB

Anxiety in a man's heart weighs it down, but a good word cheers it up.

Proverbs 12:25 HCSB

Therefore encourage one another and build each other up as you are already doing.

1 Thessalonians 5:11 HCSB

A word spoken at the right time is like golden apples on a silver tray.

Proverbs 25:11 HCSB

God has given gifts to each of you from his great variety of spiritual gifts. Manage them well so that God's generosity can flow through you.

1 Peter 4:10 NLT

Now this I say, he who sows sparingly will also reap sparingly, and he who sows bountifully will also reap bountifully. Each one must do just as he has purposed in his heart, not grudgingly or under compulsion, for God loves a cheerful giver.

2 Corinthians 9:6-7 NASB

A THOUGHT TO REMEMBER

Encouragement is the oxygen of the soul.

John Maxwell

COUNT YOUR BLESSINGS

In the space below, write down your thoughts about the power of encouragement.

_____

_____

_____

_____

_____

_____

_____

_____

_____

_____

_____

_____

_____

_____

_____

CHAPTER 17

Joy

But let all who take refuge in You rejoice.

—Psalm 5:11 HCSB

Oswald Chambers correctly observed, "Joy is the great note all throughout the Bible." C. S. Lewis echoed that thought when he wrote, "Joy is the serious business of heaven." But, even the most dedicated Christians can, on occasion, forget to celebrate each day for what it is: a priceless gift from God.

Today, let us be joyful Christians with smiles on our faces and kind words on our lips. After all, this is God's day, and He has given us clear instructions for its use. We are commanded to rejoice and be glad. So, with no further ado, let the celebration begin . . .

MORE IMPORTANT IDEAS ABOUT JOY

The Christian lifestyle is not one of legalistic do's and don'ts, but one that is positive, attractive, and joyful.

Vonette Bright

Joy is the direct result of having God's perspective on our daily lives and the effect of loving our Lord enough to obey His commands and trust His promises.

Bill Bright

Our sense of joy, satisfaction, and fulfillment in life increases, no matter what the circumstances, if we are in the center of God's will.

Billy Graham

Joy is the heart's harmonious response to the Lord's song of love.

A. W. Tozer

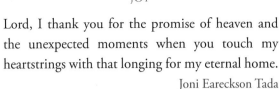

Lord, I thank you for the promise of heaven and the unexpected moments when you touch my heartstrings with that longing for my eternal home.

Joni Eareckson Tada

God knows everything. He can manage everything, and He loves us. Surely this is enough for a fullness of joy that is beyond words.

Hannah Whitall Smith

God gives to us a heavenly gift called joy, radically different in quality from any natural joy.

Elisabeth Elliot

Rejoice, the Lord is King; Your Lord and King adore! Rejoice, give thanks and sing and triumph evermore.

Charles Wesley

A life of intimacy with God is characterized by joy.

Oswald Chambers

MORE FROM GOD'S WORD

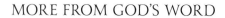

Rejoice in the Lord, you righteous ones; praise from the upright is beautiful.

Psalm 33:1 HCSB

Weeping may endure for a night, but joy comes in the morning.

Psalm 30:5 NKJV

This is the day the Lord has made; let us rejoice and be glad in it.

Psalm 118:24 HCSB

Rejoice in the Lord always. I will say it again: Rejoice!

Philippians 4:4 HCSB

But now I come to You, and these things I speak in the world, that they may have My joy fulfilled in themselves.

John 17:13 NKJV

Rejoice, and be exceeding glad: for great is your reward in heaven….

Matthew 5:12 KJV

Thou wilt show me the path of life: in thy presence is fulness of joy; at thy right hand there are pleasures for evermore.

Psalm 16:11 KJV

Delight thyself also in the LORD; and he shall give thee the desires of thine heart.

Psalm 37:4 KJV

For the Lord is good, and His love is eternal; His faithfulness endures through all generations.

Psalm 100:5 HCSB

A TIMELY TIP

Joy does not depend upon your circumstances; it depends upon your thoughts and upon your relationship with God.

COUNT YOUR BLESSINGS

In the space below, write down the things that make you joyful.

CHAPTER 18

The Simple Blessing of Patience

Rejoice in hope; be patient in affliction; be persistent in prayer.

—Romans 12:12 HCSB

Most of us are impatient for God to grant us the desires of our heart. Usually, we know what we want, and we know precisely when we want it: right now, if not sooner. But God may have other plans. And when God's plans differ from our own, we must trust in His infinite wisdom and in His infinite love.

As busy men and women living in a fast-paced world, many of us find that waiting quietly for God is difficult. Why? Because we are fallible human beings seeking to live according to our own timetables, not God's. In our better moments, we realize that patience is not only a virtue, but it is also a commandment from God.

God instructs us to be patient in all things. We must be patient with our families, our friends, and

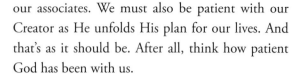

our associates. We must also be patient with our Creator as He unfolds His plan for our lives. And that's as it should be. After all, think how patient God has been with us.

MORE IMPORTANT IDEAS ABOUT PATIENCE

Those who have had to wait and work for happiness seem to enjoy it more, because they never take it for granted.

Barbara Johnson

Our challenge is to wait in faith for the day of God's favor and salvation.

Jim Cymbala

Let me encourage you to continue to wait with faith. God may not perform a miracle, but He is trustworthy to touch you and make you whole where there used to be a hole.

Lisa Whelchel

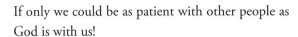

If only we could be as patient with other people as God is with us!

Jim Gallery

Teach us, O Lord, the disciplines of patience, for to wait is often harder than to work.

Peter Marshall

If you want to hear God's voice clearly and you are uncertain, then remain in His presence until He changes that uncertainty. Often much can happen during this waiting for the Lord. Sometimes he changes pride into humility; doubt into faith and peace . . . .

Corrie ten Boom

God freely admits he is holding back his power, but he restrains himself for our benefit. For all scoffers who call for direct action from the heavens, the prophets have ominous advice: Just wait.

Philip Yancey

MORE FROM GOD'S WORD

Love is patient; love is kind.

1 Corinthians 13:4 HCSB

A patient spirit is better than a proud spirit.

Ecclesiastes 7:8 HCSB

Therefore the Lord is waiting to show you mercy, and is rising up to show you compassion, for the Lord is a just God. Happy are all who wait patiently for Him.

Isaiah 30:18 HCSB

Now we exhort you, brethren, warn those who are unruly, comfort the fainthearted, uphold the weak, be patient with all.

1 Thessalonians 5:14 NKJV

A patient person [shows] great understanding, but a quick-tempered one promotes foolishness.

Proverbs 14:29 HCSB

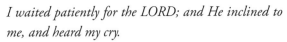

I waited patiently for the LORD; and He inclined to me, and heard my cry.

Psalm 40:1 NKJV

However, each one must live his life in the situation the Lord assigned when God called him.

1 Corinthians 7:17 HCSB

O Lord, you have examined my heart and know everything about me. You know when I sit down or stand up. You know my every thought when far away. You chart the path ahead of me and tell me where to stop and rest.

Psalm 139:1-3 NLT

A THOUGHT TO REMEMBER

Waiting is an essential part of spiritual discipline. It can be the ultimate test of faith.

Anne Graham Lotz

COUNT YOUR BLESSINGS

In the space below, write down your thoughts about the blessings that come your way when you are patient.

_____

_____

_____

_____

_____

_____

_____

_____

_____

_____

_____

_____

_____

CHAPTER 19

Finding and Keeping Happiness

How happy are those whose way is blameless, who live according to the law of the Lord! Happy are those who keep His decrees and seek Him with all their heart.

—Psalm 119:1-2 HCSB

Happiness depends less upon our circumstances than upon our thoughts. When we turn our thoughts to God, to His gifts, and to His glorious creation, we experience the joy that God intends for His children. But, when we focus on the negative aspects of life, we suffer needlessly.

Do you sincerely want to be a happy Christian? Then set your mind and your heart upon God's love and His grace. The fullness of life in Christ is available to all who seek it and claim it. Count yourself among that number. Seek first the salvation that is available through a personal relationship with Jesus Christ, and then claim the joy, the peace, and the spiritual abundance that the Shepherd offers His sheep.

MORE IMPORTANT IDEAS ABOUT HAPPINESS

People who have invested their lives in worthwhile pursuits have discovered a measure of happiness.

Warren Wiersbe

Our thoughts, not our circumstances, determine our happiness.

John Maxwell

The secret of a happy life is to delight in duty. When duty becomes delight, then burdens become blessings.

Warren Wiersbe

I am truly happy with Jesus Christ. I couldn't live without Him.

Ruth Bell Graham

Christ is the secret, the source, the substance, the center, and the circumference of all true and lasting gladness.

Mrs. Charles E. Cowman

God's goal is not to make you happy. It is to make you his.

Max Lucado

I became aware of one very important concept I had missed before: my attitude—not my circumstances—was what was making me unhappy.

Vonette Bright

We will never be happy until we make God the source of our fulfillment and the answer to our longings.

Stormie Omartian

The happiest people in the world are not those who have no problems, but the people who have learned to live with those things that are less than perfect.

James Dobson

MORE FROM GOD'S WORD

How happy is everyone who fears the Lord, who walks in His ways!

Psalm 128:1 HCSB

Happy is the man who fears the Lord, taking great delight in His commandments.

Psalm 112:1 HCSB

Happy is a man who finds wisdom and who acquires understanding.

Proverbs 3:13 HCSB

A joyful heart is good medicine, but a broken spirit dries up the bones.

Proverbs 17:22 HCSB

Happy are the people whose strength is in You, whose hearts are set on pilgrimage.

Psalm 84:5 HCSB

How happy is the man who does not follow the advice of the wicked, or take the path of sinners, or join a group of mockers!

Psalm 1:1 HCSB

If they serve Him obediently, they will end their days in prosperity and their years in happiness.

Job 36:11 HCSB

The one who understands a matter finds success, and the one who trusts in the Lord will be happy.

Proverbs 16:20 HCSB

Rejoice, and be exceeding glad: for great is your reward in heaven . . . .

Matthew 5:12 KJV

A TIMELY TIP

Don't seek happiness. Seek God's will and live it. Happiness will follow.

COUNT YOUR BLESSINGS

In the space below, write down some of the things that make you happy.

CHAPTER 20

Sharing the Gift of Kindness

And may the Lord make you increase and abound in love to one another and to all.

—1 Thessalonians 3:12 NKJV

In the busyness and confusion of daily life, it is easy to lose focus, and it is easy to become frustrated. We are imperfect human beings struggling to manage our lives as best we can, but we often fall short. When we are distracted or disappointed, we may neglect to share a kind word or a kind deed. This oversight hurts others, but it hurts us most of all.

Today, slow yourself down and be alert for those who need your smile, your kind words, or your helping hand. Make kindness a centerpiece of your dealings with others. They will be blessed, and you will be, too. When you spread a heaping helping of encouragement and hope to the world, you can't help getting a little bit on yourself.

MORE IMPORTANT IDEAS ABOUT KINDNESS

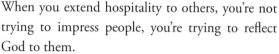

When you extend hospitality to others, you're not trying to impress people, you're trying to reflect God to them.

Max Lucado

The mark of a Christian is that he will walk the second mile and turn the other cheek. A wise man or woman gives the extra effort, all for the glory of the Lord Jesus Christ.

John Maxwell

When we do little acts of kindness that make life more bearable for someone else, we are walking in love as the Bible commands us.

Barbara Johnson

A little kindly advice is better than a great deal of scolding.

Fanny Crosby

There are many timid souls whom we jostle morning and evening as we pass them by; but if only the kind word were spoken they might become fully persuaded.

Fanny Crosby

Be so preoccupied with good will that you haven't room for ill will.

E. Stanley Jones

If we have the true love of God in our hearts, we will show it in our lives. We will not have to go up and down the earth proclaiming it. We will show it in everything we say or do.

D. L. Moody

When you launch an act of kindness out into the crosswinds of life, it will blow kindness back to you.

Dennis Swanberg

MORE FROM GOD'S WORD

Therefore, God's chosen ones, holy and loved, put on heartfelt compassion, kindness, humility, gentleness, and patience.

Colossians 3:12 HCSB

And be kind and compassionate to one another, forgiving one another, just as God also forgave you in Christ.

Ephesians 4:32 HCSB

Carry one another's burdens; in this way you will fulfill the law of Christ.

Galatians 6:2 HCSB

The cheerful heart has a continual feast.

Proverbs 15:15 NIV

Love is patient; love is kind.

1 Corinthians 13:4 HCSB

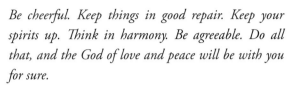

Be cheerful. Keep things in good repair. Keep your spirits up. Think in harmony. Be agreeable. Do all that, and the God of love and peace will be with you for sure.

2 Corinthians 13:11 MSG

Pure and undefiled religion before our God and Father is this: to look after orphans and widows in their distress and to keep oneself unstained by the world.

James 1:27 HCSB

See that no one renders evil for evil to anyone, but always pursue what is good both for yourselves and for all.

1 Thessalonians 5:15 NKJV

A TIMELY TIP

Kind words and good deeds have echoes that last a lifetime and beyond.

COUNT YOUR BLESSINGS

In the space below, write down your thoughts about the rewards of kindness.

_____

_____

_____

_____

_____

_____

_____

_____

_____

_____

_____

_____

_____

_____

_____

_____

CHAPTER 21

Finding Contentment

I have learned to be content in whatever circumstances I am.

—Philippians 4:11 HCSB

Everywhere we turn, or so it seems, the world promises us contentment and happiness. But the contentment that the world offers is fleeting and incomplete. Thankfully, the contentment that God offers is all encompassing and everlasting.

Happiness depends less upon our circumstances than upon our thoughts. When we turn our thoughts to God, to His gifts, and to His glorious creation, we experience the joy that God intends for His children. But, when we focus on the negative aspects of life—or when we disobey God's commandments—we cause ourselves needless suffering.

Do you sincerely want to be a contented Christian? Then set your mind and your heart upon God's love and His grace . . . and let Him take care of the rest.

MORE IMPORTANT IDEAS ABOUT CONTENTMENT

I believe that in every time and place it is within our power to acquiesce in the will of God—and what peace it brings to do so!

Elisabeth Elliot

Father and Mother lived on the edge of poverty, and yet their contentment was not dependent upon their surroundings. Their relationship to each other and to the Lord gave them strength and happiness.

Corrie ten Boom

Contentment is possible when we stop striving for more.

Charles Swindoll

Nobody who gets enough food and clothing in a world where most are hungry and cold has any business to talk about "misery."

C. S. Lewis

What a shame it will be if those who have the grace of God within them should fall short of the contentment which worldly men have attained.

C. H. Spurgeon

The happiness which brings enduring worth to life is not the superficial happiness that is dependent on circumstances. It is the happiness and contentment that fills the soul in the midst of the most distressing of circumstances.

Billy Graham

When we do what is right, we have contentment, peace, and happiness.

Beverly LaHaye

The key to contentment is to consider. Consider who you are and be satisfied with that. Consider what you have and be satisfied with that. Consider what God's doing and be satisfied with that.

Luci Swindoll

MORE FROM GOD'S WORD

A tranquil heart is life to the body, but jealousy is rottenness to the bones.

Proverbs 14:30 HCSB

But godliness with contentment is a great gain.

1 Timothy 6:6 HCSB

Let your conduct be without covetousness; be content with such things as you have. For He Himself has said, "I will never leave you nor forsake you."

Hebrews 13:5 NKJV

Rest in God alone, my soul, for my hope comes from Him.

Psalm 62:5 HCSB

So prepare your minds for service and have self-control. All your hope should be for the gift of grace that will be yours when Jesus Christ is shown to you.

1 Peter 1:13 NCV

There are different kinds of gifts, but they are all from the same Spirit. There are different ways to serve but the same Lord to serve.

1 Corinthians 12:4–5 NCV

You're blessed when you're content with just who you are—no more, no less. That's the moment you find yourselves proud owners of everything that can't be bought.

Matthew 5:5 MSG

Humble yourselves, therefore, under God's mighty hand, that he may lift you up in due time.

1 Peter 5:6 NIV

A TIMELY TIP

God offers you His peace, His protection, and His promises. If you accept these gifts, you will be content.

COUNT YOUR BLESSINGS

In the space below, write down some of the things that make you feel contented.

_____

_____

_____

_____

_____

_____

_____

_____

_____

_____

_____

_____

_____

_____

_____

CHAPTER 22

Overcoming Adversity

We are pressured in every way but not crushed; we are perplexed but not in despair.

—2 Corinthians 4:8 HCSB

From time to time, all of us face adversity, discouragement, or disappointment. And, throughout life, we must all endure life-changing personal losses that leave us breathless. When we do, God stands ready to protect us. Psalm 147 promises, "He heals the brokenhearted, and binds their wounds" (v. 3, NIV).

When we are troubled, we must call upon God, and, in His own time and according to His own plan, He will heal us.

Are you anxious? Take those anxieties to God. Are you troubled? Take your troubles to Him. Does your world seem to be trembling beneath your feet? Seek protection from the One who cannot be moved. The same God who created the universe will protect you if you ask Him . . . so ask Him.

MORE IMPORTANT IDEAS ABOUT OVERCOMING ADVERSITY

Speak the name of "Jesus," and all your storms will fold their thunderbolts and leave.

Calvin Miller

If your every human plan and calculation has miscarried, if, one by one, human props have been knocked out . . . take heart. God is trying to get a message through to you, and the message is: "Stop depending on inadequate human resources. Let me handle the matter."

Catherine Marshall

Adversity is not simply a tool. It is God's most effective tool for the advancement of our spiritual lives. The circumstances and events that we see as setbacks are oftentimes the very things that launch us into periods of intense spiritual growth. Once we begin to understand this, and accept it as a spiritual fact of life, adversity becomes easier to bear.

Charles Stanley

Oftentimes, God demonstrates His faithfulness in adversity by providing for us what we need to survive. He does not change our painful circumstances. He sustains us through them.

Charles Swindoll

The kingdom of God is a kingdom of paradox where, through the ugly defeat of a cross, a holy God is utterly glorified. Victory comes through defeat; healing through brokenness; finding self through losing self.

Chuck Colson

In order to realize the worth of the anchor, we need to feel the stress of the storm.

Corrie ten Boom

Any man can sing in the day. It is easy to sing when we can read the notes by daylight, but he is the skillful singer who can sing when there is not a ray of light by which to read. Songs in the night come only from God; they are not in the power of man.

C. H. Spurgeon

MORE FROM GOD'S WORD

*I will be with you when you pass through the waters
. . . when you walk through the fire . . . the flame will
not burn you. For I the Lord your God, the Holy One
of Israel, and your Savior.*

Isaiah 43:2-3 HCSB

*We also rejoice in our afflictions, because we know that
affliction produces endurance, endurance produces
proven character, and proven character produces hope.*

Romans 5:3-4 HCSB

*"For I know the plans I have for you"—[this is] the
Lord's declaration—"plans for [your] welfare, not for
disaster, to give you a future and a hope."*

Jeremiah 29:11 HCSB

*We know that all things work together for the good of
those who love God: those who are called according to
His purpose.*

Romans 8:28 HCSB

Dear friends, when the fiery ordeal arises among you to test you, don't be surprised by it, as if something unusual were happening to you. Instead, as you share in the sufferings of the Messiah rejoice, so that you may also rejoice with great joy at the revelation of His glory.

1 Peter 4:12-13 HCSB

But as for you, you meant evil against me; but God meant it for good, in order to bring it about as it is this day, to save many people alive.

Genesis 50:20 NKJV

Now the God of all grace, who called you to His eternal glory in Christ Jesus, will personally restore, establish, strengthen, and support you.

1 Peter 5:10 HCSB

A TIMELY TIP

When times are tough, you should guard your heart by turning it over to God.

COUNT YOUR BLESSINGS

In the space below, write down your thoughts about the ways that God continually blesses you, even when times are tough. Adversity

CHAPTER 23

The Blessing of God's Wisdom

Those who are wise shall shine like the brightness of the firmament, and those who turn many to righteousness like the stars forever and ever.

—Daniel 12:3 NKJV

Where will you place your trust today? Will you seek guidance from fallible friends and acquaintances—friends who may be well meaning but who are highly imperfect? Or will you do the smart thing by placing your faith in God's perfect wisdom? When you decide whom to trust, you will then know how best to respond to the challenges of the coming day.

Are you tired? Discouraged? Fearful? Be comforted and trust God. Are you worried or anxious? Be confident in God's power and trust His Holy Word. Are you confused? Listen to the quiet voice of your Heavenly Father. He is not a God of confusion. Talk with Him; listen to Him; trust Him. He is steadfast, and He is your Protector . . . forever.

MORE IMPORTANT IDEAS ABOUT GOD'S WISDOM

Wisdom takes us beyond the realm of mere right and wrong. Wisdom takes into account our personalities, our strengths, our weaknesses, and even our present state of mind.

Charles Stanley

All the knowledge you want is comprised in one book, the Bible.

John Wesley

A big difference exists between a head full of knowledge and the words of God literally abiding in us.

Beth Moore

Wise people listen to wise instruction, especially instruction from the Word of God.

Warren Wiersbe

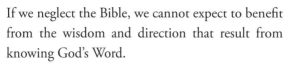

If we neglect the Bible, we cannot expect to benefit from the wisdom and direction that result from knowing God's Word.

Vonette Bright

The wonderful thing about God's schoolroom is that we get to grade our own papers. You see, He doesn't test us so He can learn how well we're doing. He tests us so we can discover how well we're doing.

Charles Swindoll

God's plan for our guidance is for us to grow gradually in wisdom before we get to the crossroads.

Bill Hybels

When terrible things happen, there are two choices, and only two: We can trust God, or we can defy Him. We believe that God is God, He's still got the whole world in His hands and knows exactly what He's doing, or we must believe that He is not God and that we are at the awful mercy of mere chance.

Elisabeth Elliot

MORE FROM GOD'S WORD

But from Him you are in Christ Jesus, who for us became wisdom from God, as well as righteousness, sanctification, and redemption.

1 Corinthians 1:30 HCSB

But also for this very reason, giving all diligence, add to your faith virtue, to virtue knowledge.

2 Peter 1:5 NKJV

Let the word of Christ dwell in you richly in all wisdom, teaching and admonishing one another in psalms and hymns and spiritual songs, singing with grace in your hearts to the Lord.

Colossians 3:16 NKJV

Trust the Lord your God with all your heart and lean not on your own understanding; in all your ways acknowledge him, and he will make your paths straight.

Proverbs 3:5-6 NIV

Pay careful attention, then, to how you walk—not as unwise people but as wise.

Ephesians 5:15 HCSB

Now if any of you lacks wisdom, he should ask God, who gives to all generously and without criticizing, and it will be given to him.

James 1:5 HCSB

Therefore, everyone who hears these words of Mine and acts on them will be like a sensible man who built his house on the rock. The rain fell, the rivers rose, and the winds blew and pounded that house. Yet it didn't collapse, because its foundation was on the rock.

Matthew 7:24-25 HCSB

A THOUGHT TO REMEMBER

To know the will of God is the greatest knowledge! To do the will of God is the greatest achievement.

George W. Truett

COUNT YOUR BLESSINGS

In the space below, write down your thoughts about the blessing of God's wisdom.

_____

_____

_____

_____

_____

_____

_____

_____

_____

_____

_____

_____

_____

_____

_____

_____

CHAPTER 24

The Blessing of Faith

For whatever is born of God overcomes the world. And this is the victory that has overcome the world—our faith.

—1 John 5:4 NKJV

Have you ever felt your faith in God slipping away? If so, you are not alone. Every life—including yours—is a series of successes and failures, celebrations and disappointments, joys and sorrows. But even when we feel very distant from God, God is never distant from us.

Jesus taught His disciples that if they had faith, they could move mountains. You can too. When you place your faith, your trust, indeed your life in the hands of Christ Jesus, you'll be amazed at the marvelous things He can do with you and through you. So strengthen your faith through praise, through worship, through Bible study, and through prayer. And trust God's plans. With Him, all things are possible, and He stands ready to open a world of possibilities to you if you have faith.

MORE IMPORTANT IDEAS ABOUT FAITH

There are a lot of things in life that are difficult to understand. Faith allows the soul to go beyond what the eyes can see.

John Maxwell

The popular idea of faith is of a certain obstinate optimism: the hope, tenaciously held in the face of trouble, that the universe is fundamentally friendly and things may get better.

J. I. Packer

I am truly grateful that faith enables me to move past the question of "Why?"

Zig Ziglar

Just as our faith strengthens our prayer life, so do our prayers deepen our faith. Let us pray often, starting today, for a deeper, more powerful faith.

Shirley Dobson

I'm convinced that there is nothing that can happen to me in this life that is not precisely designed by a sovereign Lord to give me the opportunity to learn to know Him.

Elisabeth Elliot

Faith is seeing light with the eyes of your heart, when the eyes of your body see only darkness.

Barbara Johnson

Forgive us our lack of faith, lest ulcers become our badge of disbelief.

Peter Marshall

If God chooses to remain silent, faith is content.

Ruth Bell Graham

Faith is trusting in advance what will only make sense in reverse.

Phillip Yancey

MORE FROM GOD'S WORD

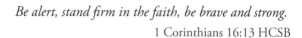

Be alert, stand firm in the faith, be brave and strong.

1 Corinthians 16:13 HCSB

For we walk by faith, not by sight.

2 Corinthians 5:7 HCSB

I have fought a good fight, I have finished my course, I have kept the faith.

2 Timothy 4:7 KJV

Now faith is the reality of what is hoped for, the proof of what is not seen.

Hebrews 11:1 HCSB

Now without faith it is impossible to please God, for the one who draws near to Him must believe that He exists and rewards those who seek Him.

Hebrews 11:6 HCSB

Trust in the Lord with all your heart, and do not rely on your own understanding; think about Him in all your ways, and He will guide you on the right paths.

Proverbs 3:5-6 HCSB

For the eyes of the Lord range throughout the earth to show Himself strong for those whose hearts are completely His.

2 Chronicles 16:9 HCSB

He granted their request because they trusted in Him.

1 Chronicles 5:20 HCSB

A TIMELY TIP

Faith should be practiced more than studied. Vance Havner said, "Nothing is more disastrous than to study faith, analyze faith, make noble resolves of faith, but never actually to make the leap of faith." How true!

COUNT YOUR BLESSINGS

In the space below, write down your thoughts about the importance of faith.

_____

_____

_____

_____

_____

_____

_____

_____

_____

_____

_____

_____

_____

_____

_____

_____

The Blessing of Friendship

I give thanks to my God for every remembrance of you.
—Philippians 1:3 HCSB

Friend: a one-syllable word describing "a person who is attached to another by feelings of affection or personal regard." This definition, or one very similar to it, can be found in any dictionary, but genuine friendship is much more. When we examine the deeper meaning of friendship, so many descriptors come to mind: trustworthiness, loyalty, helpfulness, kindness, understanding, forgiveness, encouragement, humor, and cheerfulness, to mention but a few.

Genuine friendship should be treasured and nurtured. As Christians, we are commanded to love one another. The familiar words of 1 Corinthians 13:2 remind us that love and charity are among God's greatest gifts: "And though I have the gift of prophecy, and understand all mysteries, and all knowledge; and though I have all faith, so that I could remove mountains, and have not charity, I am nothing" (KJV).

Today and every day, resolve to be a trustworthy, encouraging, loyal friend. And, treasure the people in your life who are loyal friends to you. Friendship is, after all, a glorious gift, praised by God. Give thanks for that gift and nurture it.

MORE IMPORTANT IDEAS ABOUT THE BLESSING OF FRIENDSHIP

Live in the present and make the most of your opportunities to enjoy your family and friends.

Barbara Johnson

God often keeps us on the path by guiding us through the counsel of friends and trusted spiritual advisors.

Bill Hybels

Do you want to be wise? Choose wise friends.

Charles Swindoll

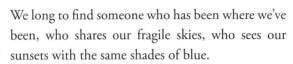

We long to find someone who has been where we've been, who shares our fragile skies, who sees our sunsets with the same shades of blue.

Beth Moore

Friendship is one of the sweetest joys of life. Many might have failed beneath the bitterness of their trial had they not found a friend.

C. H. Spurgeon

Yes, the Spirit was sent to be our Counselor. Yes, Jesus speaks to us personally. But often he works through another human being.

John Eldredge

Whenever we develop significant friendships with those who are not like us culturally, we become broader, wiser persons.

Richard Foster

A friend is one who makes me do my best.

Oswald Chambers

MORE FROM GOD'S WORD

A friend loveth at all times, and a brother is born for adversity.

Proverbs 17:17 KJV

Oil and incense bring joy to the heart, and the sweetness of a friend is better than self-counsel.

Proverbs 27:9 HCSB

Beloved, if God so loved us, we also ought to love one another.

1 John 4:11 NKJV

Thine own friend, and thy father's friend, forsake not....

Proverbs 27:10 KJV

The one who loves his brother remains in the light, and there is no cause for stumbling in him.

1 John 2:10 HCSB

All bitterness, anger and wrath, insult and slander must be removed from you, along with all wickedness. And be kind and compassionate to one another, forgiving one another, just as God also forgave you in Christ.

Ephesians 4:31-32 HCSB

If a brother or sister is without clothes and lacks daily food, and one of you says to them, "Go in peace, keep warm, and eat well," but you don't give them what the body needs, what good is it?

James 2:15–16 HCSB

A THOUGHT TO REMEMBER

Perhaps the greatest treasure on earth and one of the only things that will survive this life is human relationships: old friends. We are indeed rich if we have friends. Friends who have loved us through the problems and heartaches of life. Deep, true, joyful friendships. Life is too short and eternity too long to live without old friends.

Gloria Gaither

COUNT YOUR BLESSINGS

In the space below, write down your thoughts about the blessing of friendship.

CHAPTER 26

The Blessing of Time

He said to them, "It is not for you to know times or periods that the Father has set by His own authority."
—Acts 1:7 HCSB

Time is a nonrenewable gift from God. But sometimes, we treat our time here on earth as if it were not a gift at all: We may be tempted to invest our lives in trivial pursuits and petty diversions. But our Father beckons each of us to a higher calling.

An important element of our stewardship to God is the way that we choose to spend the time He has entrusted to us. Each waking moment holds the potential to do a good deed, to say a kind word, or to offer a heartfelt prayer. Our challenge, as believers, is to use our time wisely in the service of God's work and in accordance with His plan for our lives.

Each day is a special treasure to be savored and celebrated. May we—as Christians who have so much to celebrate—never fail to praise our Creator by rejoicing in His glorious creation and by using it wisely.

MORE IMPORTANT IDEAS ABOUT THE GIFT OF TIME

Our time is short! The time we can invest for God, in creative things, in receiving our fellowmen for Christ, is short!

Billy Graham

As we surrender the use of our time to the lordship of Christ, He will lead us to use it in the most productive way imaginable.

Charles Stanley

By his wisdom, he orders his delays so that they prove to be far better than our hurries.

C. H. Spurgeon

God's silence is in no way indicative of His activity or involvement in our lives. He may be silent, but He is not still.

Charles Swindoll

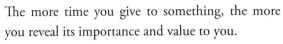

The more time you give to something, the more you reveal its importance and value to you.

Rick Warren

God has a present will for your life. It is neither chaotic nor utterly exhausting. In the midst of many good choices vying for your time, He will give you the discernment to recognize what is best.

Beth Moore

Our leisure, even our play, is a matter of serious concern. There is no neutral ground in the universe: every square inch, every split second, is claimed by God and counterclaimed by Satan.

C. S. Lewis

When we read of the great Biblical leaders, we see that it was not uncommon for God to ask them to wait, not just a day or two, but for years, until God was ready for them to act.

Gloria Gaither

MORE FROM GOD'S WORD

Therefore humble yourselves under the mighty hand of God, that He may exalt you in due time.

1 Peter 5:6 NKJV

I wait for the Lord, my soul waits, and in His word I do hope. My soul waits for the Lord more than those who watch for the morning—Yes, more than those who watch for the morning.

Psalm 130:5-6 NKJV

He has made everything appropriate in its time. He has also put eternity in their hearts, but man cannot discover the work God has done from beginning to end.

Ecclesiastes 3:11 HCSB

But those who wait on the LORD shall renew their strength; they shall mount up with wings like eagles, they shall run and not be weary, they shall walk and not faint.

Isaiah 40:31 NKJV

For My thoughts are not your thoughts, and your ways are not My ways. For as heaven is higher than earth, so My ways are higher than your ways, and My thoughts than your thoughts.

Isaiah 55:8-9 HCSB

However, each one must live his life in the situation the Lord assigned when God called him.

1 Corinthians 7:17 HCSB

The Lord is my rock, my fortress and my savior; my God is my rock in whom I find protection. He is my shield, the strength of my salvation, and my stronghold.

Psalm 18:2 NLT

A THOUGHT TO REMEMBER

Overcommitment and time pressures are the greatest destroyers of marriages and families. It takes time to develop any friendship, whether with a loved one or with God himself.

James Dobson

COUNT YOUR BLESSINGS

In the space below, write down your thoughts about the gift of time.

_____

_____

_____

_____

_____

_____

_____

_____

_____

_____

_____

_____

_____

_____

_____

_____

_____

CHAPTER 27

Blessed by the Right Kind of Attitude

Set your minds on what is above, not on what is on the earth.

—Colossians 3:2 HCSB

How will you direct your thoughts today? Will you obey the words of Philippians 4:8 by dwelling upon those things that are honorable, true, and worthy of praise? Or will you allow your thoughts to be hijacked by the negativity that seems to dominate our troubled world? Are you fearful, angry, bored, or worried? Are you so preoccupied with the concerns of this day that you fail to thank God for the promise of eternity? Are you confused, bitter, or pessimistic? If so, God wants to have a little talk with you.

God intends that you experience joy and abundance, but He will not force His joy upon you; you must claim it for yourself. So, today and every day hereafter, celebrate this life that God has given you by focusing your thoughts and your energies upon "whatever is of good repute." Today, count your blessings instead of your hardships. And thank the Giver of all things good for gifts that are simply too numerous to count.

MORE IMPORTANT IDEAS ABOUT YOUR ATTITUDE

A positive attitude will have positive results because attitudes are contagious.

Zig Ziglar

The people whom I have seen succeed best in life have always been cheerful and hopeful people who went about their business with a smile on their faces.

Charles Kingsley

Life goes on. Keep on smiling and the whole world smiles with you.

Dennis Swanberg

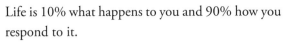

Life is 10% what happens to you and 90% how you respond to it.

Charles Swindoll

Outlook determines outcome and attitude determines action.

Warren Wiersbe

Your attitude, not your aptitude, will determine your altitude.

Zig Ziglar

I became aware of one very important concept I had missed before: my attitude—not my circumstances—was what was making me unhappy.

Vonette Bright

The Reference Point for the Christian is the Bible. All values, judgments, and attitudes must be gauged in relationship to this Reference Point.

Ruth Bell Graham

MORE FROM GOD'S WORD

For the word of God is living and powerful, and sharper than any two-edged sword, piercing even to the division of soul and spirit, and of joints and marrow, and is a discerner of the thoughts and intents of the heart.

Hebrews 4:12 NKJV

Thanks be to God for His indescribable gift.

2 Corinthians 9:15 HCSB

And let the peace of the Messiah, to which you were also called in one body, control your hearts. Be thankful.

Colossians 3:15 HCSB

Finally brothers, whatever is true, whatever is honorable, whatever is just, whatever is pure, whatever is lovely, whatever is commendable—if there is any moral excellence and if there is any praise—dwell on these things.

Philippians 4:8 HCSB

My cup runs over. Surely goodness and mercy shall follow me all the days of my life; and I will dwell in the house of the Lord forever.

Psalm 23:5-6 NKJV

The Lord is my light and my salvation; whom shall I fear? The Lord is the strength of my life; of whom shall I be afraid?

Psalm 27:1 KJV

The Lord says, "I will make you wise and show you where to go. I will guide you and watch over you."

Psalm 32:8 NCV

Give thanks to the Lord, for He is good; His faithful love endures forever.

Psalm 118:29 HCSB

A TIMELY TIP

A positive attitude leads to positive results; a negative attitude leads elsewhere.

COUNT YOUR BLESSINGS

In the space below, write down your thoughts about
the rewards of a positive attitude.

_____

_____

_____

_____

_____

_____

_____

_____

_____

_____

_____

_____

_____

_____

_____

CHAPTER 28

Compassionate Christianity

And let us be concerned about one another in order to promote love and good works.

—Hebrews 10:24 HCSB

Concentration camp survivor Corrie ten Boom correctly observed, "The measure of a life is not its duration but its donation." These words remind us that the quality of our lives is determined not by what we are able to take from others, but instead by what we are able to share with others.

God's Word commands us to be compassionate, generous servants to those who need our support. As believers, we have been richly blessed by our Creator. We, in turn, are called to share our gifts, our possessions, our testimonies, and our talents.

The thread of compassion is woven into the very fabric of Christ's teachings. If we are to be disciples of Christ, we, too, must be zealous in caring

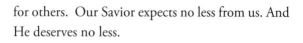

for others. Our Savior expects no less from us. And He deserves no less.

MORE IMPORTANT IDEAS ABOUT COMPASSION

Before you can dry another's tears, you too must weep.

Barbara Johnson

Our Lord worked with people as they were, and He was patient—not tolerant of sin, but compassionate.

Vance Havner

In terms of ministry, people are everything to us because they are everything to Christ.

Beth Moore

When action-oriented compassion is absent, it's a tell-tale sign that something's spiritually amiss.

Bill Hybels

Deep in the dark night of the suffering soul comes a moment when nothing intellectual or psychological matters. It is the time of the touch, the tender touch, a hand held, a cheek kissed, a holy embrace that conveys more to the human spirit than anything from tongue or pen.

Bill Bright

We must learn to regard people less in the light of what they do or do not do, and more in the light of what they suffer.

Dietrich Bonhoeffer

It's not difficult to make an impact on your world. All you really have to do is put the needs of others ahead of your own. You can make a difference with a little time and a big heart.

James Dobson

Ministry is not something we do for God; it is something God does in and through us.

Warren Wiersbe

MORE FROM GOD'S WORD

Therefore, God's chosen ones, holy and loved, put on heartfelt compassion, kindness, humility, gentleness, and patience.

Colossians 3:12 HCSB

Finally, all of you be of one mind, having compassion for one another; love as brothers, be tenderhearted, be courteous.

1 Peter 3:8 NKJV

Brethren, if anyone among you wanders from the truth, and someone turns him back, let him know that he who turns a sinner from the error of his way will save a soul from death and cover a multitude of sins.

James 5:19-20 NKJV

As each one has received a gift, minister it to one another, as good stewards of the manifold grace of God.

1 Peter 4:10 NKJV

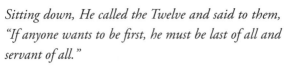

Sitting down, He called the Twelve and said to them, "If anyone wants to be first, he must be last of all and servant of all."

Mark 9:35 HCSB

Dear friend, you are showing your faith by whatever you do for the brothers, and this you are doing for strangers.

3 John 1:5 HCSB

In every way I've shown you that by laboring like this, it is necessary to help the weak and to keep in mind the words of the Lord Jesus, for He said, "It is more blessed to give than to receive."

Acts 20:35 HCSB

A TIMELY TIP

God has given you countless blessings . . . and He wants you to share them.

COUNT YOUR BLESSINGS

In the space below, write down your thoughts about
the importance of compassion.

_____

_____

_____

_____

_____

_____

_____

_____

_____

_____

_____

_____

_____

_____

CHAPTER 29

The Blessing of God's Word

Heaven and earth will pass away, but My words will never pass away.

—Matthew 24:35 HCSB

The Psalmist describes God's Word as, "a light to my path." Is the Bible your lamp? If not, you are depriving yourself of a priceless gift from the Creator. Vance Havner observed, "It takes calm, thoughtful, prayerful meditation on the Word to extract its deepest nourishment." And make no mistake: you need that kind of nourishment.

Are you a woman who trusts God's Word without reservation? Hopefully so, because the Bible is unlike any other book—it is a guidebook for life here on earth and for life eternal.

God's Word can be a light to guide your steps. Claim it as your light today, tomorrow, and every day of your life—and then walk confidently in the footsteps of God's only begotten Son.

MORE IMPORTANT IDEAS ABOUT GOD'S WORD

Anything that comes to us from the God of the Word will deepen our love for the Word of God.

A. W. Tozer

Nobody ever outgrows Scripture; the book widens and deepens with our years.

C. H. Spurgeon

God's voice isn't all that difficult to hear. He sometimes shouts through our pain, whispers to us while we're relaxing on vacation, occasionally, He sings to us in a song, and warns us through the sixty-six books of His written Word. It's right there, ink on paper. Count on it—that book will never lead you astray.

Charles Swindoll

The Scriptures were not given for our information, but for our transformation.

D. L. Moody

Just as you do not analyze the words of someone you love, but accept them as they are said to you, accept the Word of Scripture and ponder it in your heart.

Dietrich Bonhoeffer

The Bible is God's Word, given to us by God Himself so we can know Him and His will for our lives.

Billy Graham

The Gospel is not so much a demand as it is an offer, an offer of new life to man by the grace of God.

E. Stanley Jones

God's Word is a light not only to our path but also to our thinking. Place it in your heart today, and you will never walk in darkness.

Joni Eareckson Tada

MORE FROM GOD'S WORD

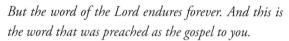

But the word of the Lord endures forever. And this is the word that was preached as the gospel to you.

1 Peter 1:25 HCSB

All Scripture is inspired by God and is profitable for teaching, for rebuking, for correcting, for training in righteousness, so that the man of God may be complete, equipped for every good work.

2 Timothy 3:16-17 HCSB

For the word of God is living and effective and sharper than any two-edged sword, penetrating as far as to divide soul, spirit, joints, and marrow; it is a judge of the ideas and thoughts of the heart.

Hebrews 4:12 HCSB

The one who is from God listens to God's words. This is why you don't listen, because you are not from God.

John 8:47 HCSB

For I am not ashamed of the gospel, because it is God's power for salvation to everyone who believes.

Romans 1:16 HCSB

Man shall not live by bread alone, but by every word that proceeds from the mouth of God.

Matthew 4:4 NKJV

Like newborn infants, desire the unadulterated spiritual milk, so that you may grow by it in your salvation.

1 Peter 2:2 HCSB

Worship the Lord your God and . . . serve Him only.

Matthew 4:10 HCSB

A THOUGHT TO REMEMBER

If we are not continually fed with God's Word, we will starve spiritually.

Stormie Omartian

COUNT YOUR BLESSINGS

In the space below, write down your thoughts about the rewards of studying God's Word.

_____

_____

_____

_____

_____

_____

_____

_____

_____

_____

_____

_____

_____

_____

_____

CHAPTER 30

Celebrating the Simple Blessings

This is the day the LORD has made; we will rejoice and be glad in it.

—Psalm 118:24 NKJV

The 118th Psalm reminds us that today, like every other day, is a cause for celebration. God gives us this day; He fills it to the brim with possibilities, and He challenges us to use it for His purposes. The day is presented to us fresh and clean at midnight, free of charge, but we must beware: Today is a non-renewable resource—once it's gone, it's gone forever. Our responsibility, of course, is to use this day in the service of God's will and according to His commandments.

Today, treasure the time that God has given you. Give Him the glory and the praise and the thanksgiving that He deserves. And search for the hidden possibilities that God has placed along your path. This day is a priceless gift from God, so use it joyfully and encourage others to do likewise. After all, this is the day the Lord has made . . . .

MORE IMPORTANT IDEAS ABOUT CELEBRATION

Joy is the direct result of having God's perspective on our daily lives and the effect of loving our Lord enough to obey His commands and trust His promises.

Bill Bright

Our sense of joy, satisfaction, and fulfillment in life increases, no matter what the circumstances, if we are in the center of God's will.

Billy Graham

He wants us to have a faith that does not complain while waiting, but rejoices because we know our times are in His hands—nail-scarred hands that labor for our highest good.

Kay Arthur

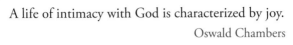

A life of intimacy with God is characterized by joy.

Oswald Chambers

Lord, I thank you for the promise of heaven and the unexpected moments when you touch my heartstrings with that longing for my eternal home.

Joni Eareckson Tada

God knows everything. He can manage everything, and He loves us. Surely this is enough for a fullness of joy that is beyond words.

Hannah Whitall Smith

God gives to us a heavenly gift called joy, radically different in quality from any natural joy.

Elisabeth Elliot

When we get rid of inner conflicts and wrong attitudes toward life, we will almost automatically burst into joy.

E. Stanley Jones

MORE FROM GOD'S WORD

Rejoice in the Lord always. I will say it again: Rejoice!

Philippians 4:4 HCSB

David and the whole house of Israel were celebrating before the Lord.

2 Samuel 6:5 HCSB

Their sorrow was turned into rejoicing and their mourning into a holiday. They were to be days of feasting, rejoicing, and of sending gifts to one another and the poor.

Esther 9:22 HCSB

At the dedication of the wall of Jerusalem, they sent for the Levites wherever they lived and brought them to Jerusalem to celebrate the joyous dedication with thanksgiving and singing accompanied by cymbals, harps, and lyres.

Nehemiah 12:27 HCSB

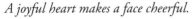

A joyful heart makes a face cheerful.

Proverbs 15:13 HCSB

Make me hear joy and gladness.

Psalm 51:8 NKJV

Let us hold on to the confession of our hope without wavering, for He who promised is faithful.

Hebrews 10:23 HCSB

May the God of hope fill you with all joy and peace as you trust in him, so that you may overflow with hope by the power of the Holy Spirit.

Romans 15:13 NIV

A TIMELY TIP

God has given you the gift of life (here on earth) and the promise of eternal life (in heaven). Now, He wants you to celebrate those gifts. By celebrating the gift of life, you protect your heart from the dangers of pessimism, regret, hopelessness, and bitterness.

COUNT YOUR BLESSINGS

In the space below, write down some of the blessings you should celebrate today.

_____

_____

_____

_____

_____

_____

_____

_____

_____

_____

_____

_____

_____

_____

CHAPTER 31

Finding Purpose

Whatever you do, do all to the glory of God.
—1 Corinthians 10:31 NKJV

Life is best lived on purpose, not by accident—the sooner we discover what God intends for us to do with our lives, the better. But the search to find meaning and purpose for our lives is seldom easy. Sometimes we wander aimlessly in a wilderness of our own making. And sometimes, we must try—and fail—many times before we discover our life's work.

Mother Teresa observed, "We are all pencils in the hand of God." And Willa Cather noted, "This is happiness: to be dissolved in something complete and great." How true.

Today is a wonderful day to "dissolve yourself" in something important. You can do it—and if you get busy, you will.

MORE IMPORTANT IDEAS ABOUT FINDING PURPOSE

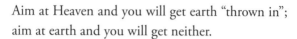

Aim at Heaven and you will get earth "thrown in"; aim at earth and you will get neither.

C. S. Lewis

God custom-designed you with your unique combination of personality, temperament, talents, and background, and He wants to harness and use these in His mission to reach this messed-up world.

Bill Hybels

We aren't just thrown on this earth like dice tossed across a table. We are lovingly placed here for a purpose.

Charles Swindoll

Blessed are those who know what on earth they are here on earth to do and set themselves about the business of doing it.

Max Lucado

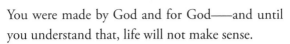

You were made by God and for God——and until you understand that, life will not make sense.

Rick Warren

Whatever purpose motivates your life, it must be something big enough and grand enough to make the investment worthwhile.

Warren Wiersbe

We set our eyes on the finish line, forgetting the past, and straining toward the mark of spiritual maturity and fruitfulness.

Vonette Bright

A fish would never be happy living on land, because it was made for water. An eagle could never feel satisfied if it wasn't allowed to fly. You will never feel completely satisfied on earth, because you were made for more.

Rick Warren

MORE FROM GOD'S WORD

For it is God who is working among you both the willing and the working for His good purpose.

Philippians 2:13 HCSB

We know that all things work together for the good of those who love God: those who are called according to His purpose.

Romans 8:28 HCSB

I will instruct you and show you the way to go; with My eye on you, I will give counsel.

Psalm 32:8 HCSB

You reveal the path of life to me; in Your presence is abundant joy; in Your right hand are eternal pleasures.

Psalm 16:11 HCSB

Commit your activities to the Lord and your plans will be achieved.

Proverbs 16:3 HCSB

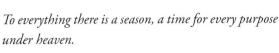

To everything there is a season, a time for every purpose under heaven.

Ecclesiastes 3:1 NKJV

People may make plans in their minds, but the Lord decides what they will do.

Proverbs 16:9 NCV

Yet Lord, You are our Father; we are the clay, and You are our potter; we all are the work of Your hands.

Isaiah 64:8 HCSB

Lord, You are my lamp; the Lord illuminates my darkness.

2 Samuel 22:29 HCSB

A TIMELY TIP

When you gain a clear vision of your purpose for life here on earth—and for life everlasting—your steps will be sure.

COUNT YOUR BLESSINGS

In the space below, jot down a few ideas about the direction God is leading you during this phase of your journey.

_____

_____

_____

_____

_____

_____

_____

_____

_____

_____

_____

_____

_____

_____

_____

CHAPTER 32

Count Your Blessings and Be Thankful

In everything give thanks; for this is the will of God in Christ Jesus for you.

—1 Thessalonians 5:18 NKJV

As we begin each day, we should pause to consider God's blessings. God's gifts are, of course, too numerous to count, but as believers, we should attempt to count them nonetheless. Our blessings include life, friends, family, talents, opportunities, and possessions, for starters.

The Greek biographer Plutarch observed, "The worship most acceptable to God comes from a thankful and cheerful heart."

And Marianne Williamson correctly observed, "Joy is what happens to us when we allow ourselves to recognize how good things really are."

So today, as a way of saying thanks to God, the Giver of all things good, praise His gifts, use His gifts, and share His gifts. God certainly deserves your gratitude, and you certainly deserve the experience of being grateful.

MORE IMPORTANT IDEAS ABOUT PRAISE AND THANKSGIVING

God is worthy of our praise and is pleased when we come before Him with thanksgiving.

Shirley Dobson

The act of thanksgiving is a demonstration of the fact that you are going to trust and believe God.

Kay Arthur

Thanksgiving is good but Thanksliving is better.

Jim Gallery

Thank God every morning when you get up that you have something to do that day which must be done, whether you like it or not.

Charles Kingsley

The joy of God is experienced as I love, trust, and obey God—no matter the circumstances—and as I allow Him to do in and through me whatever He wishes, thanking Him that in every pain there is pleasure, in every suffering there is satisfaction, in every aching there is comfort, in every sense of loss there is the surety of the Savior's presence, and in every tear there is the glistening eye of God.

Bill Bright

Praise and thank God for who He is and for what He has done for you.

Billy Graham

It is always possible to be thankful for what is given rather than to complain about what is not given. One or the other becomes a habit of life.

Elisabeth Elliot

It is only with gratitude that life becomes rich.

Dietrich Bonhoeffer

MORE FROM GOD'S WORD

Thanks be to God for His indescribable gift.

2 Corinthians 9:15 HCSB

And let the peace of the Messiah, to which you were also called in one body, control your hearts. Be thankful.

Colossians 3:15 HCSB

Therefore as you have received Christ Jesus the Lord, walk in Him, rooted and built up in Him and established in the faith, just as you were taught, and overflowing with thankfulness.

Colossians 2:6-7 HCSB

Enter his gates with thanksgiving, go into his courts with praise. Give thanks to him and bless his name.

Psalm 100:4 NLT

It is good to give thanks to the Lord, and to sing praises to Your name, O Most High.

Psalm 92:1 NKJV

And whatever you do, in word or in deed, do everything in the name of the Lord Jesus, giving thanks to God the Father through Him.

Colossians 3:17 HCSB

Everything created by God is good, and nothing is to be rejected, if it is received with gratitude; for it is sanctified by means of the word of God and prayer.

1 Timothy 4:4-5 NASB

Therefore, since we receive a kingdom which cannot be shaken, let us show gratitude, by which we may offer to God an acceptable service with reverence and awe . . . .

Hebrews 12:28 NASB

A THOUGHT TO REMEMBER

You owe God everything . . . including your thanks.

COUNT YOUR BLESSINGS

In the space below, write down a few of the things you're thankful for today.

_____

_____

_____

_____

_____

_____

_____

_____

_____

_____

_____

_____

_____

CHAPTER 33

The Ultimate Blessing: God's Son

But whoever keeps His word, truly in him the love of God is perfected. This is how we know we are in Him: the one who says he remains in Him should walk just as He walked.

—1 John 2:5-6 HCSB

Hannah Whitall Smith spoke to believers of every generation when she advised, "Keep your face upturned to Christ as the flowers do to the sun. Look, and your soul shall live and grow." That's powerful advice. When we turn our hearts to Jesus, we receive His blessings, His peace, and His grace.

Do you regularly take time each day to embrace Christ's love? Do you prayerfully ask God to lead you in the footsteps of His Son? And are you determined to obey God's Word even if the world encourages you to do otherwise? If so, you'll soon experience the peace and the power that flows freely from the Son of God.

MORE IMPORTANT IDEAS ABOUT FOLLOWING CHRIST

Living life with a consistent spiritual walk deeply influences those we love most.

Vonette Bright

The cross that Jesus commands you and me to carry is the cross of submissive obedience to the will of God, even when His will includes suffering and hardship and things we don't want to do.

Anne Graham Lotz

We have in Jesus Christ a perfect example of how to put God's truth into practice.

Bill Bright

A disciple is a follower of Christ. That means you take on His priorities as your own. His agenda becomes your agenda. His mission becomes your mission.

Charles Stanley

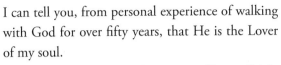

I can tell you, from personal experience of walking with God for over fifty years, that He is the Lover of my soul.

Vonette Bright

Peter said, "No, Lord!" But he had to learn that one cannot say "No" while saying "Lord" and that one cannot say "Lord" while saying "No."

Corrie ten Boom

Christ is not valued at all unless He is valued above all.

St. Augustine

When we truly walk with God throughout our day, life slowly starts to fall into place.

Bill Hybels

Identification with the death of Jesus Christ means identification with Him to the death of everything that was never in Him.

Oswald Chambers

MORE FROM GOD'S WORD

We encouraged, comforted, and implored each one of you to walk worthy of God, who calls you into His own kingdom and glory.

1 Thessalonians 2:12 HCSB

Therefore as you have received Christ Jesus the Lord, walk in Him.

Colossians 2:6 HCSB

I, therefore, the prisoner in the Lord, urge you to walk worthy of the calling you have received.

Ephesians 4:1 HCSB

If we live by the Spirit, we must also follow the Spirit.

Galatians 5:25 HCSB

"Follow Me," Jesus told them, "and I will make you into fishers of men!" Immediately they left their nets and followed Him.

Mark 1:17-18 HCSB

For whoever wants to save his life will lose it, but whoever loses his life because of Me and the gospel will save it.

Mark 8:35 HCSB

In the beginning was the Word, and the Word was with God, and the Word was God . . . . And the Word was made flesh, and dwelt among us, (and we beheld his glory, the glory as of the only begotten of the Father,) full of grace and truth.

John 1:1, 14 KJV

The next day John saw Jesus coming toward him and said, "Here is the Lamb of God, who takes away the sin of the world!"

John 1:29 HCSB

A TIMELY TIP

If you sincerely wish to follow in Christ's footsteps, welcome Him into your heart, obey His commandments, and share His never-ending love.

COUNT YOUR BLESSINGS

In the space below, write down your thoughts about the meaning of Christ's sacrifice and the blessing of His love.

_____

_____

_____

_____

_____

_____

_____

_____

_____

_____

_____

_____

_____